RECEIVING
GOD'S
PROMISES

INHERITING OUR EARTHLY AND
HEAVENLY BLESSINGS
IN CHRIST

DEREK PRINCE

WHITAKER
HOUSE

Publisher's Note: This book was compiled from the extensive archive of Derek Prince's unpublished materials and approved by the Derek Prince Ministries editorial team.

Scripture quotations marked (NASB) are taken from the *New American Standard Bible*®, NASB®, © 1960, 1962, 1963, 1968, 1971, 1972, 1973, 1975, 1977 by The Lockman Foundation. Used by permission. (www.Lockman.org). Scripture quotations marked (NKJV) are taken from the *New King James Version*, © 1979, 1980, 1982 by Thomas Nelson, Inc. Used by permission. All rights reserved. Scripture quotations marked (NIV) are taken from the *Holy Bible, New International Version*®, NIV®, © 1973, 1978, 1984 by the International Bible Society. Used by permission of Zondervan. All rights reserved. Scripture quotations marked (KJV) are taken from the King James Version of the Holy Bible. Scripture quotations taken from the *King James Easy Read Bible*, KJVER®, are © 2001, 2007, 2010, 2015 by Whitaker House. Used by permission. All rights reserved.

Personal pronouns and adjectives relating to God, Jesus, and the Holy Spirit in Scripture quotations from the *New International Version* and King James Version have been capitalized to correspond to the overall style used in this book. The forms LORD and GOD (in small caps) in Bible quotations represent the Hebrew name for God *Yahweh* (Jehovah), while *Lord* and *God* normally represent the name *Adonai*, in accordance with the Bible version used.

Boldface type in the Scripture quotations indicates the author's emphasis.

RECEIVING GOD'S PROMISES:
Inheriting Our Earthly and Heavenly Blessings in Christ
Revised and Updated Edition

Derek Prince Ministries
P.O. Box 19501 ✦ Charlotte, North Carolina 28219-9501
www.derekprince.org

ISBN: 978-1-64123-973-8 ✦ eBook 978-1-62911-992-2
Printed in Colombia
© 2018, 2023 by Derek Prince Ministries–International

Whitaker House
1030 Hunt Valley Circle ✦ New Kensington, PA 15068
www.whitakerhouse.com

Library of Congress Control Number: 2023931273

1 2 3 4 5 6 7 8 9 10 11 ⓌⒽ 30 29 28 27 26 25 24 23

CONTENTS

PART THREE: APPLYING GOD'S PROMISES

BIBLE PROMISES BY TOPIC

INTRODUCTION: CLAIMING OUR INHERITANCE

Imagine that a rather official-looking registered letter is delivered to you by the postal carrier. Upon opening it, you discover that the letter is from an attorney in a faraway city, informing you that a distant relative has died and left you a substantial inheritance. This inheritance will allow you to retire, live very comfortably for the rest of your life, and provide a secure financial future for your children. Upon receiving such a letter, most people would immediately drop whatever they were doing, catch the earliest flight, and head directly to the attorney's office to claim their inheritance!

If that entire process sounds wonderful to you, then I have some very good news. A relative of yours *has* died, and in His last will and testament, He has left you a fabulous inheritance. In fact, He has left you an entire kingdom! That relative's name is Jesus, and in His will (which we call the New Testament), He has set forth the riches that are yours—if you will take the time and effort to receive and claim them.

The New Testament is the charter of the Christian faith. When we use the word *testament*, we are using it in the same sense in which we use the phrase "the last will and testament of so-and-so." In other words, by employing the word *testament*, we indicate that something has been bequeathed to us through the death of another.

The New Testament reveals to you and me the tremendous inheritance that has been made available to us through the death of Jesus on our behalf. *It announces that we are heirs of a kingdom.* Unfortunately, many Christians have never discovered what their real inheritance is or how to take possession of it. They are like the individual who receives notice that he or she is the heir to a tremendous fortune but never takes any steps to find out what the inheritance is or how to claim it.

It is my hope that through this book, you will discover your inheritance as a Christian and learn how you—as a rightful heir of the kingdom of God—can receive God's promises and begin to claim your earthly and heavenly blessings in Christ.

PART ONE:

THE GREAT EXCHANGE

1

A KINGDOM TRANSFER

FROM DARKNESS TO LIGHT

As we begin to explore the topic of receiving God's promises by discovering and claiming our God-given inheritance, let's revisit the imaginary scenario I described in the introduction to this book. After receiving the news about your amazing inheritance, your next question would naturally be, "Where do I need to go in order to claim it?" Discovering *where* your inheritance is would be the first practical step toward taking possession of it. Likewise, as Christians, you and I need to ask, "Where is my inheritance?"

To answer this question, we will first turn to the words of the apostle Paul in Colossians 1:12–14.

> *Giving thanks to the Father, who has qualified us* [or "made us capable"] *to share in the inheritance of the saints in light.*
> (Colossians 1:12 NASB)

In this verse, Paul is speaking of an inheritance that is reserved for God's people. It is an inheritance "*in light.*" He then goes on to explain what must happen for us to take possession of that inheritance.

> For He [God the Father] *delivered us from the domain of darkness, and transferred us to the kingdom of His beloved Son, in whom we have redemption, the forgiveness of sins.*
>
> (Colossians 1:13–14 NASB)

Here Paul gives us a picture of two kingdoms: the kingdom of darkness and the kingdom of light. The kingdom of light is the kingdom of God and His Son, Jesus Christ. The kingdom of darkness is Satan's kingdom. These two kingdoms are in absolute opposition to one another.

Now let's go back to the question "Where is my inheritance?" Our inheritance is located in the kingdom of light. But in order for us to be able to gain our inheritance, we must first be delivered from the domain of darkness—that is, from Satan's power over us and our lives.

This deliverance comes about through the redemption God has provided for us by the death of Jesus on the cross. By means of this redemption, we receive forgiveness for our sins. Once we are forgiven, Satan has *no more legal claim over us.* We are set free from his domain, and we are made capable of entering into our inheritance in the kingdom of light.

To many people, all this may sound like simple, basic truth. However, we must understand something about the dilemma of being in the kingdom of darkness. When people are in the dark, they cannot see their true condition. This applies to all people who are under Satan's domain—they are in the dark, and therefore they cannot perceive the actual situation they are in. Each of us needs a light to penetrate our darkness.

Where can we find light that powerful? We find it in the gospel—revealed in the Word of God. Consider what the Bible tells us about our true condition before Christ forgave and redeemed us. Paul vividly describes our darkened state in the second chapter of his letter to the Ephesians:

> *And you were dead in your trespasses and sins* [we were not physically dead but spiritually dead, alienated and cut off from the life that is in God], *in which* [trespasses and sins] *you formerly walked according to the course of this world, according to the prince of the power of the air, of the spirit that is now working in the sons of disobedience.*
>
> (Ephesians 2:1–2 NASB)

In the kingdom of darkness, in our trespasses and sins, we were actually under the dominion of a spiritual power. That spiritual entity is called *"the prince of the power of the air,"* which is described as *"the spirit that is now working in the sons of disobedience."* Our disobedience to God automatically exposed us to the influence and domination of Satan. Paul then goes on to say that this was the universal condition of every human being, including you and me:

> *Among them we too all formerly lived in the lusts of our flesh, indulging the desires of the flesh and of the mind, and were by nature children of wrath, even as the rest.*
>
> (Ephesians 2:3 NASB)

OUT OF BONDAGE

Again, what Paul says in the above passage is true of all of us. In our natural condition, we are at enmity with God. We are alienated from Him. We are in the dark, and we are captivated by the desires of our flesh and our mind. Consequently, through these evil, ungodly desires, we are held in bondage by Satan, the prince of darkness.

God's purpose through the gospel is to deliver us from that bondage of Satan and darkness. By the power of the gospel, He brings us into our inheritance in the kingdom of light. This truth is very clearly stated by Paul in the book of Acts, where he quotes the commission he received from Jesus Christ to carry the gospel to the Gentile world:

> "...*to open their eyes so that they may turn from darkness to light and from the dominion of Satan to God, in order that they may receive forgiveness of sins and an inheritance among those who have been sanctified by faith in Me.*"
>
> (Acts 26:18 NASB)

We clearly see that God's ultimate purpose is for us to receive forgiveness of sins so we can thus be qualified for our inheritance in the kingdom of light. But before this can happen, He must open our eyes to our true condition. He must turn us from darkness to light—from submission to Satan and his dominion to obedience to God and His kingdom.

We can draw a very important conclusion from the above Scriptures and from our own experience: darkness has power. The power of Satan is real. He is not imaginary. He is not a theological fantasy. Satan is a real being with real power who, in fact, cruelly dominates those who are alienated from God. Therefore, in order to enter God's kingdom, we must first be delivered from the power of Satan.

RANSOMED!

This deliverance from the power of Satan has been made possible *only* through the redemption provided for us by the death of Jesus on our behalf. We need to understand more precisely the meaning of the word *redemption*. It comes from a verb, *to redeem*, which means "to buy back" or "to ransom."

Here is an example of what such redemption signifies. Suppose the son of a wealthy man were to be taken by kidnappers who held him for ransom. If the wealthy father was willing to pay the ransom demanded by the kidnappers, and his son was restored to him, we could say that by paying the demanded price, that wealthy father had "redeemed" his son from the kidnappers.

In a very similar manner, Jesus has paid the price to redeem us from the kingdom of Satan. In Romans 7:14, Paul writes,

For we know that the Law is spiritual, but I am carnal, sold under sin.   (NKJV)

When Paul uses the phrase *"sold under sin,"* he is employing an illustrative picture taken from the ancient Roman world. In Roman times, when a person was sold in the slave market, he or she was said to be "sold under the spear." The slave was placed on a stand against a post, from which a spear hung over the slave's head. The evidence that the person was being sold as a slave was that he or she was standing under this outstretched spear.

Paul is saying that we, through our sin, were exposed as slaves in Satan's slave market. The spear stretched out over our head was the sin we had committed. Our sin made us slaves for sale, *"sold under sin."*

When people were sold as slaves, they had no choice as to what their occupations would be. Some slaves might be compelled to take quite a respectable occupation, like housekeeping or teaching; others might be made to perform a very menial occupation, like cleaning latrines; still others might be forced into an immoral role, such as that of a prostitute. The person who was a slave had no choice. It was solely the choice of the one who owned him or her.

And so it is with us as sinners. We are all slaves of Satan by nature. Some of us are respectable sinners; some of us are less respectable sinners. However, there is really no ultimate difference between the two. We are sinners nonetheless. Yet when Jesus came to earth, He walked into Satan's slave market and saw us there for sale. It was Jesus who paid the price to buy us out of that bondage—and out from under Satan's dominion.

THE PRICELESS BLOOD

What was the price Jesus paid for our redemption? His precious blood. Paul writes,

> *In Him* [Christ] *we have redemption through His blood, the forgiveness of our trespasses, according to the riches of His grace.*   (Ephesians 1:7 NASB)

Our redemption was paid for by the blood of Jesus. That is what obtained the forgiveness of our sins. Jesus bore the penalty in our place on the cross. Why? So that we might be forgiven and thus be qualified to inherit the kingdom of *"the saints in light"* (Colossians 1:12 NASB). The truth of our redemption through Jesus's blood is also stated elsewhere in the New Testament in a very beautiful passage:

> *If you address as Father the One who impartially judges according to each man's work, conduct yourselves in fear during the time of your stay upon earth; knowing that you were not redeemed with perishable things like silver or gold from your futile way of life inherited from your forefathers, but with precious blood, as of a lamb unblemished and spotless, the blood of Christ.*   (1 Peter 1:17–19 NASB)

It was the priceless blood that Jesus shed on our behalf that paid the price of our redemption. His blood delivered us from Satan's slave market and the kingdom of darkness. His blood obtained for us the forgiveness of sins and qualified us to enter *"the inheritance of the saints in light"* (Colossians 1:12 NASB).

In the next chapter, we will take a closer look at what Jesus accomplished on our behalf on the cross. We will learn more about our transfer from Satan's kingdom of darkness and our qualification to enter into our inheritance in God's kingdom of light.

INHERITING THE BLESSINGS

In Him [Christ] *we have redemption through His blood, the forgiveness of our trespasses, according to the riches of His grace.*   (Ephesians 1:7 NASB)

Giving thanks to the Father, who has qualified us [or "made us capable"] *to share in the inheritance of the saints in light.*   (Colossians 1:12 NASB)

2

FROM CURSE TO BLESSING

Since the fall of mankind, all the inhabitants of the earth have been caught in a cosmic tug-of-war. The conflict is between two great opposing kingdoms: the kingdom of light, which is the realm of God and His Son, Jesus Christ—and the kingdom of darkness, which is the domain of Satan. As we saw in the previous chapter, through sin and disobedience against God, we became *"carnal, sold under sin"* (Romans 7:14 NKJV), thus becoming slaves to *"the law of sin and death"* (Romans 8:2 NASB). We were put up for sale in Satan's slave market.

We have also already seen that God, in His mercy, provided a way for us to be delivered from the kingdom of darkness and to become heirs of the kingdom of light. Jesus came into Satan's slave market and paid the price of our redemption with His blood. He paid the full penalty due for all our sins and disobedience so that we might be forgiven.

THE SECRET OF THE CROSS

Let us further examine the nature and scope of our marvelous redemption through Christ's work on the cross. We will begin by reading these words of Paul in the third chapter of Galatians:

> *Christ redeemed us* [notice the word *"redeemed"*] *from the curse of the Law, having become a curse for us—for it is written, "Cursed is everyone who hangs on a tree"—in order that in Christ Jesus the blessing of Abraham might come to the Gentiles, so that we might receive the promise of the Spirit through faith.* (Galatians 3:13–14 NASB)

Here Paul is referring to a Scripture passage in the Law of Moses in which God declares that everyone who is put to death by hanging on a tree is under a curse. (See Deuteronomy 21:22–23.) The evidence that such people are under a curse is that they are hanging visibly on a piece of wood—and that includes the piece of wood that made the cross on which Christ was crucified.

In order to redeem us from the curse of the Law, Christ became a curse for us. This was visibly demonstrated when He hung on the cross of Calvary. It was necessary for Christ to become a curse, because the curse of God is imposed against all sin and disobedience against Him.

The secret of what took place on the cross is this: *there was a divinely ordained exchange.* This was something that could not be seen by the natural eye. Rather, it could be perceived only by the revelation of God through the Holy Spirit and through Scripture. The exchange was this: Christ became a curse. He took the curse due to our disobedience so we might receive the blessing of God through faith in Him—the blessing Jesus earned for us by His obedience.

THE SERVANT WITH NO NAME

The exchange that took place on the cross is more fully pictured in Isaiah 53. In this chapter, Isaiah the prophet speaks of a nameless servant. However, all the writers of the New Testament unanimously identify this servant as the Messiah, Jesus of Nazareth. In verses 4–6, which is the very heart of Isaiah 53 and of this revelation, we read the following words, beginning with verse 4:

> *Surely He [Jesus] took up our infirmities and carried our sorrows [more literally, "our pains"], yet we considered Him stricken by God, smitten by Him, and afflicted.*
>
> (Isaiah 53:4 NIV)

It is remarkable that Isaiah uses the term "*we.*" This reference is primarily to the Jewish people, but it includes the whole human race. "*We considered Him stricken by God, smitten by Him, and afflicted.*"

Years ago, in Israel, I was talking with a Jewish man, telling him of my belief that Jesus is the Messiah. I vividly remember his comment at the time, because his response was remarkable to me. He said, "I can't believe that Jesus was a righteous man, because if He had been, God would not have allowed Him to die such a death. It must have been the judgment of God upon Him."

This man's statement was exactly what Isaiah is saying in this passage: "*We considered Him stricken by God, smitten by Him.*" But in the next two verses, Isaiah goes on to point out *why* Jesus suffered. It was not for His sins (because He had none), but for ours.

> *But He was pierced for our transgressions, He was crushed for our iniquities; the punishment that brought us peace was upon Him, and by His wounds we are healed. We all, like sheep, have gone astray, each of us has turned to his own way; and the* LORD *has laid on Him the iniquity of us all.*
>
> (Isaiah 53:5–6 NIV)

A TOTAL EXCHANGE

The provision Jesus made for us on the cross was spiritual and physical. The exchange pictured in Isaiah 53 includes these two components. Spiritually, *"He was pierced for our transgressions, He was crushed for our iniquities"* (verse 5 NIV). Transgressions and iniquities are spiritual. We could translate them as "acts of disobedience" and "acts of rebellion." Jesus bore the punishment due to our acts of disobedience and rebellion so we, in turn, might be reconciled to God and thus have peace. That is the spiritual aspect of the exchange.

On the physical side, Jesus took our infirmities and carried our pains. (See Isaiah 53:4.) The result is that we are healed, or, more literally, healing has been obtained for us. That is the physical aspect of the exchange. Once more, there was a complete exchange on the cross, both spiritually and physically. Jesus took the evil that is due us, so we might receive the good that is due Him.

The basic problem of the human race is stated by Isaiah in the sixth verse of this passage: *"Each of us has turned to his own way"* (NIV, NASB). That is the universal guilt of all humanity. Thankfully, few of us have committed all the specific sins, such as murder, adultery, or theft. There is one problem, however, of which we are all guilty: *each of us has turned to his or her own way.* Each of us is guilty of stubbornness, disobedience, and rebellion. That is the root problem of the human race—and that is the problem Jesus dealt with by His death on the cross on our behalf. In the original Hebrew, the last part of verse 6 signifies, "The Lord *made to meet upon Him* the rebellion of us all." Rebellion and all its evil consequences met together that day upon Jesus as He hung on the cross.

THE CURSE THAT FOLLOWS

We need to understand that throughout the history of the human race, sin and disobedience against God have always brought a curse. The first example in human history is found in Genesis 3, which records the temptation of Adam and Eve by Satan (who was disguised as a serpent) and their subsequent fall into sin. Their disobedience was disclosed, and God pronounced judgment on it.

This is what He said to the guilty parties (notice the recurrence of the word *"cursed"*):

> *The* LORD *God said to the serpent, "Because you have done this, cursed are you more than all cattle, and more than every beast of the field; on your belly shall you go, and dust shall you eat all the days of your life...." To the woman He said, "I will greatly multiply your pain in childbirth, in pain you shall bring forth children; yet your desire shall be for your husband, and he shall rule over you." Then to Adam He said, "Because you have listened to the voice of your wife, and have eaten from the tree about which I commanded you, saying, 'You shall not eat from it'; cursed is the ground because of you; in toil you shall eat of it all the days of your life."*
>
> (Genesis 3:14, 16–17 NASB)

As soon as sin entered the human race, it was followed by the curse. The curse descended upon the serpent and upon the ground. The result for Adam and Eve was toil and pain. All these are the outworkings of the curse brought upon humanity by our sin.

TWO OPPOSITE POSSIBILITIES

The principle that disobedience against God always brings a curse is more fully expressed in the Law of Moses in Deuteronomy 28. This chapter sets forth two opposite possibilities: (1) the blessings that will come upon us if we walk in humility and obedience toward God; (2) the curses that will come upon us if we walk in stubbornness, pride, and disobedience toward God. These two alternatives are set forth for us very clearly. Let's read the words of Moses in the first two verses of Deuteronomy 28:

> *Now it shall be, if you will diligently obey the* LORD *your God, being careful to do all His commandments which I command you today, the* LORD *your God will set you high above all the*

*nations of the earth. And all these blessings shall come upon
you and overtake you, if you will obey the LORD your God.*
(Deuteronomy 28:1–2 NASB)

Please notice that when we walk in obedience, we do not need
to pursue the blessings of God; *the blessings of God overtake us!*
Blessing naturally results from obedience to God. In fact, God has
ordered the universe according to that law.

Next, Moses presents the opposite side of the picture—the
results of disobedience:

*But it shall come about, if you will not obey the LORD your
God, to observe to do all His commandments and His statutes
with which I charge you today, that all these curses shall come
upon you and overtake you.* (Deuteronomy 28:15 NASB)

Moses then outlines a very long and detailed list of curses. If
we were to study this chapter in more detail, we would find that
both the blessings and the curses cover the three main areas of
life: spiritual, physical, and material. Likewise, the full outworking of redemption through Jesus Christ covers these three main
areas.

In 3 John 2, we see a very beautiful picture of redemption and
its results. In this verse, John writes to his friend Gaius,

*Beloved, I pray that in all respects you may prosper and be in
good health, just as your soul prospers.* (NASB)

In this complete prayer, John prays that his friend may
prosper materially and financially, and also be in good health,
even as his soul prospers. Once more, we see the three areas
mentioned above—spiritual, physical, and material. In the following three chapters, we will consider each of these areas in
more detail.

INHERITING THE BLESSINGS

Beloved, I pray that in all respects you may prosper and be in good health, just as your soul prospers.   (3 John 2 NASB)

Christ redeemed us from the curse of the Law, having become a curse for us—for it is written, "Cursed is everyone who hangs on a tree"—in order that in Christ Jesus the blessing of Abraham might come to the Gentiles, so that we might receive the promise of the Spirit through faith.

(Galatians 3:13–14 NASB)

3

SPIRITUAL BENEFITS OF REDEMPTION

We ended the previous chapter on a redemptive note. So far, we have seen that God has made a way for us to be delivered from the slavery of the kingdom of darkness and to claim our rightful inheritance in the kingdom of light. The specific way God has provided is through the death of Jesus Christ on the cross.

We have also learned the secret of what took place on the cross: *a divinely ordained exchange.* Jesus took upon Himself the curses that are due to us for our disobedience. These curses encompass the whole realm of the kingdom of darkness. Jesus took these curses so that we, in turn, might enter into the blessings that are due to Jesus—earned by His obedience. These blessings embrace the whole area of the kingdom of light. Both the curses and the blessings are worked out in three major realms of our lives: spiritual, physical, and material.

In this chapter, we will focus on the spiritual area of life. What are the spiritual curses from which Christ has delivered us? And what are the spiritual blessings which Christ has made available to us?

To answer these questions, we will again refer to Deuteronomy 28, the chapter that sets out in great detail two opposite outcomes: the blessings that result from obedience to God and the curses that result from disobedience to Him. However, let's begin by noting the basic causes that bring either blessings or curses into our lives.

WHAT CAUSES BLESSINGS AND CURSES?

I am going to quote from the same passage we looked at in the last chapter, but in place of the word "*obey,*" I am going to use an alternate translation found in the margin of the *New American Standard Bible.* This rendering is more literal than the wording in the actual text of that Bible version because it is closer to the original Hebrew. We will first identify the causes of blessings, starting in Deuteronomy 28:1–2, incorporating the translation from the marginal note in brackets:

> *Now it shall be, if you will diligently [listen to the voice of] the LORD your God, being careful to do all His commandments which I command you today, the LORD your God will set you high above all the nations of the earth. And all these blessings shall come upon you and overtake you, if you will [listen to the voice of] the LORD your God.* (NASB)

Then, in verse 15, Moses turns to the curses. This is the reason the curses come:

> *But it shall come about, if you will not [listen to the voice of] the LORD your God, to observe to do all His commandments and His statutes with which I charge you today, that all these curses shall come upon you and overtake you.* (NASB)

It is vital to understand the decisive difference between earning the blessings and earning the curses. It is summed up in one short but very important phrase: *listening to God's voice.* "*If you will diligently* [listen to the voice of] *the LORD your God,...all these blessings shall come upon you,*" but "*if you will **not** [listen to the voice of] the LORD your God,...all these curses shall come upon you.*"

AVOIDING SPIRITUAL DANGER

Can you see how crucial this issue is? Our whole destiny for well-being or for disaster is settled by the voice to which we listen. Listening to the voice of the Lord and obeying what He says will bring blessing. But not listening to the voice of the Lord will bring a curse—actually, many curses. Of course, it is not sufficient to listen to the voice of the Lord unless we also obey what He says. But, conversely, it is impossible to obey what God says unless we first hear His voice, because it is His voice that tells us what He requires us to do.

The great spiritual danger that confronts so many professing Christians is this: they have become insensitive to the voice of God. They might continue in their religious activities and duties, but their Christian life has become routine and formal, simply a pattern of habits they have cultivated. They don't have an ongoing, continuous awareness of God's voice. Yet, in all of God's dealings with His people throughout history, His primary requirement has been *that we listen to His voice.*

This truth is stated clearly by the Lord in Jeremiah 7:22–23:

> *For I did not speak to your fathers, or command them in the day that I brought them out of the land of Egypt, concerning burnt offerings and sacrifices. But this is what I commanded them, saying, "Obey My voice, and I will be your God, and you will be My people; and you will walk in all the way which I command you, that it may be well with you."*
>
> (Jeremiah 7:22–23 NASB)

In these verses, God explains that what He really desired of the Israelites when He redeemed them out of Egypt was not that they keep the Law for the offering of sacrifices but that they listen to

His voice. His voice would lead them to keep the Law and to offer righteous sacrifices. Merely observing the externals of the Law by offering the sacrifices was of no avail to them if they were not doing it as a result of listening to the voice of the Lord. Remember, the key requirement of God is this: *that we listen to His voice.*

HEARING AND FOLLOWING

"*Obey My voice*" (Jeremiah 7:23 NASB) is therefore the Lord's simple requirement of us in order that He may be our God, and we may be His people. That sums it up as simply as possible. Some people might think the requirement is different in the New Testament, but it is not. The principle is exactly the same. Jesus clearly states this truth in a single verse:

> *My sheep hear My voice, and I know them, and they follow Me.*   (John 10:27 NASB)

What is the mark that we really belong to Jesus? Is it that we practice a certain pattern of life or that we hold to a certain set of doctrines? No. The mark of those who are truly His is that they hear His voice, and, hearing His voice, they follow Him. Hearing and following is the mark of true believers in every era, of every race and culture, and in all denominations and church traditions. It is not something external—it is an inner personal relationship with the Lord that enables us to hear His voice and, hearing His voice, to follow where He leads us. The simple pathway to God's blessings is to hear and obey His voice, but the inevitable end of not hearing and obeying God's voice is a sure path to curses.

CURSES OF THE INNER PERSONALITY

Next, I will briefly list the curses that affect us in the spiritual realm, or the inner realm of our personality, as they are listed by Moses in Deuteronomy 28 (NASB). These curses all result from disobedience to God:

In verse 20, Moses says that we will experience *"confusion...in all* [we] *undertake to do."* That is the first specific spiritual curse—confusion. We can easily see that much of the modern world is full of confusion.

In verse 28, Moses lists *"madness and...bewilderment of heart"* as results of not hearing God's voice. These, too, are curses.

Verse 34 says, *"You shall be driven mad by the sight of what you see."* We might say that mental and emotional breakdown is a curse. In some cases, it can be the result of disobedience against God. It has been my observation that one of the most common causes of confusion and mental and emotional breakdown is involvement in the occult. This is due to wrong spiritual relationships and participation in activities that are forbidden by the Word of God.

Then, in verse 65, Moses speaks of *"a trembling heart...and despair of soul."*

I believe we could sum up these spiritual consequences of disobedience with words like *confusion, frustration, inner agony,* and *torment.* These are serious problems that, throughout the span of my ministry, I have continually encountered in the lives of people in every nation.

BLESSINGS OF THE INNER PERSONALITY

On the other hand, there are countless blessings in the inner realm of the spirit that result from obedience. I believe they may be summed up in one short, beautiful word: *peace.* In Isaiah 53:5, picturing the exchange that took place when Jesus died on the cross, Isaiah writes, *"The punishment that brought us peace was upon Him"* (NIV). Jesus endured the judgment and punishment that were due us because of our sin and disobedience, so we might be reconciled with God. And once reconciled with God, so we might be delivered from inner agony and torment, from confusion and frustration, and know the reality of a deep, settled, inward peace. From personal experience in my own life, that kind of deep, settled peace is not merely a theory, a doctrine, or a theology—it is a reality.

There are two Scriptures in the New Testament that speak of such peace. The first is from Romans:

> *Therefore having been justified by faith, we have peace with God through our Lord Jesus Christ.* (Romans 5:1 NASB)

"We have peace with God." What wonderful words! No longer are we guilty. No longer do we have to fear that somehow we are not pleasing God. We have peace with Him.

The second is this beautiful verse from Philippians, which describes the experiential results of peace within us:

> *The peace of God, which transcends all understanding, will guard your hearts and your minds in Christ Jesus.*
> (Philippians 4:7 NIV)

In our contemporary culture, it takes the peace of God to guard our hearts and minds. I can testify that God's peace can do that. The Hebrew word translated *"peace"* (*shalom*) means more than just the absence of conflict; it means "wholeness" or "well-being." God's peace, which begins in the inner man, leads to total well-being. It works not just in the spiritual realm of our lives, but also in the physical and material realms, as we will see in the next chapters.

INHERITING THE BLESSINGS

> *Therefore having been justified by faith, we have peace with God through our Lord Jesus Christ.* (Romans 5:1 NASB)

> *The peace of God, which transcends all understanding, will guard your hearts and your minds in Christ Jesus.*
> (Philippians 4:7 NIV)

4

PHYSICAL BENEFITS
OF REDEMPTION

Through His death on our behalf, Jesus purchased two great benefits for us: one "negative," in the sense that we were taken out of something, and one "positive," in which we gained access to something. On the negative side, Jesus delivered us from the kingdom of darkness. On the positive side, Jesus opened for us a complete inheritance in the kingdom of light. A divinely ordained exchange through the cross made this possible. Jesus took upon Himself the curses due us because of our disobedience, so we might, in turn, inherit the blessings earned by His obedience. Again, the curses and blessings involved in this exchange cover three main areas: spiritual, physical, and material.

Earlier, we opened up our study of Deuteronomy 28, the great chapter in the Bible that lists both the blessings for obedience and the curses for disobedience. It also informs us of the basic causes of both blessings and curses: *listening to the Lord's voice brings blessings; not listening to the Lord's voice brings curses.* This principle runs all through Scripture. Our entire destiny ultimately rests on this fulcrum: whether or not we listen to the voice of the Lord and then do what He says.

If we do not listen to His voice, we cannot do what He says. We must have a living, ongoing personal relationship with the Lord that enables us to hear His voice. As Jesus said, *"My sheep hear My voice,...and they follow Me"* (John 10:27 NASB). The mark of true believers in every era is that they hear the voice of Jesus, and they follow Him. Hearing brings blessings; refusing to hear brings curses.

CURSES OF THE PHYSICAL REALM

We have previously looked at the impact of blessings and curses on our inner spiritual reality. In this chapter, we will examine how blessings and curses affect the physical realm of our lives. I want to briefly summarize some of the physical curses that result from not hearing and not obeying the voice of the Lord. Bear in mind that the curses on this list from Deuteronomy 28 (NASB) *do not* belong to the redeemed people of God.

Verse 21: *"The LORD will make the pestilence cling to you."*

Verse 22: *"The LORD will smite you with consumption and with fever and with inflammation."*

Verse 27: *"The LORD will smite you with...boils...and with tumors* [hemorrhoids] *and with the scab and with the itch."*

Verse 28: *"The LORD will smite you with...blindness."*

Verse 35: *"The LORD will strike you on the knees and legs with sore boils,...from the sole of your foot to the crown of your head."*

Verse 59 is amazing in its explicit statement of all the physical disasters that result from disobedience:

Then the LORD will bring extraordinary plagues on you and your descendants, even severe and lasting plagues, and miserable and chronic sicknesses.

So many Christians are enduring curses when they should be enjoying blessings. Why would we experience the curses? Probably for two main reasons: either because we do not know they are curses, or we do not realize that Jesus has delivered us from the curses so we might inherit the blessings instead.

In verse 60, God speaks about *"all the diseases of Egypt."* I spent two years in Egypt as a soldier in the British Army during World War II, and I can attest that the diseases of Egypt were then extremely numerous. In fact, I would say that most types of disease are found in some form in Egypt. However, the curse of diseases for disobedience extends even further, because verse 61 says, *"Also every sickness and every plague which, not written in the book of this law, the LORD will bring on you...."* Logically, therefore, every kind of sickness and every kind of plague is a curse. And somehow or other, the ultimate cause of disease is rooted in disobedience against God.

REDEEMED FROM PHYSICAL CURSES

The prophet Isaiah gives us a vivid description of the results of disobedience and rebellion. Speaking to the nation of Israel, he compares the people's condition, as the result of their disobedience, to that of a body that is completely sick.

Why should you be beaten anymore? Why do you persist in rebellion? Your whole head is injured, your whole heart afflicted. From the sole of your foot to the top of your head there is no soundness—only wounds and welts and open sores, not cleansed or bandaged or soothed with oil.

(Isaiah 1:5–6 NIV)

These verses from Isaiah provide a striking metaphor of the results of disobedience. Yet as I was reading this passage one day, the Holy Spirit showed me something wonderful and beautiful about it. I saw that not merely is it a metaphor of the condition of Israel due to their disobedience, but it is also a literal picture of Jesus as He hung on the cross. Consider these phrases again:

"Why should you be beaten anymore?" Jesus was beaten with the Roman scourge—with its fearful nine thongs, each one studded with bone or metal. (See, for example, Matthew 27:26.)

"Your whole head is injured." Remember the thorns that were pressed down upon His head? (See, for example, Matthew 27:29.)

"Your whole heart [is] afflicted." I believe Jesus actually died of a broken heart.

"From the sole of your foot to the top of your head there is no soundness—only wounds and welts and open sores, not cleansed or bandaged or soothed with oil." This is an exact description of Jesus as He hung upon the cross. He was in that condition because He redeemed us from the curse, being made a curse for us. All those physical curses that are a result of our disobedience against God came upon Jesus on the cross.

PHYSICAL BLESSINGS

Now that we have examined in some detail the physical curses that come from disobedience—the ones Jesus bore in His own body—let's proceed to look at the physical blessings that Jesus purchased for us at Calvary. We refer to Isaiah 53:4–5:

> *Surely He [Jesus] took up our infirmities and carried our sorrows [pains], yet we considered Him stricken by God, smitten by Him, and afflicted. But He was pierced for our transgressions, He was crushed for our iniquities; the punishment that*

*brought us peace was upon Him, and by His wounds we are
healed.* (NIV)

Please notice that Jesus took the physical consequences of disobedience so we might receive healing. The phrase at the end of verse 5, *"by His wounds we are healed,"* is more literally translated from the Hebrew as, "by His wounds it was healed for us." We could say it this way: "By His wounds, healing was obtained for us." Healing was made our inheritance through the wounds Jesus bore on His body.

This passage from Isaiah is quoted in the New Testament in chapter 8 of Matthew's gospel. Describing the ministry of Jesus in healing the sick and casting out evil spirits, Matthew writes:

*When evening had come, they brought to Him many who were
demon-possessed; and He cast out the spirits with a word, and
healed all who were ill in order that what was spoken through
Isaiah the prophet might be fulfilled, saying, "He Himself took
our infirmities, and carried away our diseases."*

(Matthew 8:16–17 NASB)

Matthew leaves no doubt about the identity of the Person who has fulfilled the prophecies of Isaiah 53. He applies these verses directly to Jesus. Also, Matthew—being a Jew—understood the Hebrew language. Therefore, he had no doubt that the application of those verses in Isaiah 53 was to the physical body. It was the physical healing of the sick that was the fulfillment of the prophecy given in Isaiah.

AN ETERNAL WORK

Why was Jesus able to heal all who were sick? Because, in the eternal purposes of God, He was to bear our infirmities and carry away our diseases. In a certain sense, the cross is eternal. Although Jesus's work on the cross had not yet been fulfilled when Isaiah 53 was written, in God's sight, it was already accomplished. Jesus was "*the Lamb slain from the foundation of the world*" (Revelation 13:8 NKJV). God identified the coming sacrifice with the ministry of Jesus and gave His seal of blessing upon it in the healing of the sick.

When Jesus answered His critics for healing a man on the Sabbath, He said,

> *If a man receives circumcision on the Sabbath that the Law of Moses may not be broken, are you angry with Me because I made an entire man well on the Sabbath?* (John 7:23 NASB)

Notice, Jesus makes the "*entire man*" well. Every area of human existence and human personality can be healed through Jesus.

Likewise, after being the instrument through which God healed the lame man at the Beautiful Gate, Peter declared,

> *By faith in the name of Jesus, this man whom you see and know was made strong. It is Jesus' name and the faith that comes through Him that has given this complete healing to him, as you can all see.* (Acts 3:16 NIV)

This man's healing was "*complete.*" That is the physical outworking of the redemption provided for us by Jesus. You and I can be grateful for the work of physicians, psychiatrists, and other medical professionals. But there is only one Person in the universe who can say, "I make an entire man well! I can deal with all his problems: spiritual, mental, emotional, and physical." That Person is the Lord Jesus Christ.

Let's conclude this chapter by considering a beautiful verse from the book of Hebrews:

> *Jesus Christ is the same yesterday and today, yes and forever.* (Hebrews 13:8 NASB)

Today, as we look to Jesus by faith on the basis of His redemption, we can know that the same results that took place in the ministry of Jesus and the apostles, as recorded in the New Testament, are available to you and me. They can come to us right now through faith in Jesus.

INHERITING THE BLESSINGS

Surely He [Jesus] took up our infirmities and carried our sorrows [pains], yet we considered Him stricken by God, smitten by Him, and afflicted. But He was pierced for our transgressions, He was crushed for our iniquities; the punishment that brought us peace was upon Him, and by His wounds we are healed. (Isaiah 53:4–5 NIV)

By faith in the name of Jesus, this man whom you see and know was made strong. It is Jesus' name and the faith that comes through Him that has given this complete healing to him, as you can all see. (Acts 3:16 NIV)

5

MATERIAL BENEFITS
OF REDEMPTION

I hope you are beginning to get a glimpse of the glorious inheritance secured for us by Jesus's immeasurable sacrifice of Himself on Calvary. In the past few chapters, we have discussed the profound exchange that took place on the cross. Jesus received in His physical body the curses due to us so we might gain the blessings He earned by His obedience.

MATERIAL BLESSINGS

Having seen the curses for disobedience and the blessings through redemption made available to us in the physical realm, we now want to consider the curses and blessings that pertain to the material realm. In this chapter, we will look first at the many material blessings promised to obedience, as recorded for us by Moses in Deuteronomy 28 (NASB):

Verse 3: *"Blessed shall you be in the city, and blessed shall you be in the country."*

Verse 4: *"Blessed shall be the offspring of your body and the produce of your ground and the offspring of your beasts, the increase of your herd and the young of your flock."* Crops and cattle were the main material possessions of the Israelites as an agricultural community.

Verse 5: *"Blessed shall be your basket and your kneading bowl."* Today, we might say, "Blessed shall be your shopping basket" or "...your wallet."

Verse 8: *"The LORD will command the blessing upon you in your barns and in all that you put your hand to, and He will bless you in the land which the LORD your God gives you."* I love the thought that God is going to *command* His blessing upon us. God will bless *"all that you put your hand to."* He leaves absolutely nothing out of anything that we undertake!

Verse 11: *"The LORD will make you abound in prosperity, in the offspring of your body and in the offspring of your beast and in the produce of your ground, in the land which the LORD swore to your fathers to give you."* Notice the phrase *"the LORD will make you abound in prosperity."* Abundant prosperity is a blessing that results from hearing and obeying the voice of the Lord.

Moses returns briefly to the same theme in the next chapter of Deuteronomy, where he says, *"So keep the words of this covenant to do them, that you may prosper in all that you do"* (Deuteronomy 29:9 NASB). Keeping the words of God's covenant causes us to prosper in everything we do. That leaves no room for failure or frustration in any area of our lives.

MATERIAL CURSES

Clearly, God commands abundant material blessings if His people will listen to His voice and obey Him. However, there are material curses for disobedience. We see the evidence for this in Deuteronomy 28:29:

And you shall grope at noon, as the blind man gropes in dark-ness, and you shall not prosper in your ways....   (NASB)

This describes a total inability to find the right way through life. Notice that just as abounding in prosperity is a blessing, not prospering in our ways is a curse. Moses restates this truth more completely and vividly later in Deuteronomy 28, where the blessing and the curse are set directly side by side:

Because you did not serve the LORD your God with joy and a glad heart, for the abundance of all things; therefore you shall serve your enemies whom the LORD shall send against you, in hunger, in thirst, in nakedness, and in the lack of all things; and He will put an iron yoke on your neck until He has destroyed you.   (Deuteronomy 28:47–48 NASB)

It is God's will that we serve Him *"with joy and a glad heart, for the abundance of all things."* Abundance will be the outcome of our obedience to His will. But the alternative for those who will not serve the Lord *"with joy and a glad heart"* is very grim. You could not have the two alternatives more clearly contrasted than in these two verses. The results of obedience? *"The abundance of all things."* The results of disobedience? Serving one's enemies *"in hunger, in thirst, in nakedness, and in the lack of all things."*

ABSOLUTE POVERTY

"In hunger, in thirst, in nakedness, and in the lack of all things." Once, when I was meditating on these words, I saw that Deuteronomy 28:48 is a description of absolute poverty. The person depicted is hungry but has nothing to eat, thirsty but has nothing to drink, naked but has no clothes to wear—a person in lack of all things. Is it possible to picture greater poverty than that—hunger, thirst, nakedness, and the lack of all things?

It is very important for us to see that poverty is a curse. Poverty is not a mark of holiness, as some religious traditions have taught or implied. If it takes poverty to make you and me holy, I question how holy we really are! Poverty is a curse—and it does not belong to the people of God.

What joy and release came into my own soul when I saw so clearly that poverty is not for the redeemed children of God! For the Lord's redeemed people, the will of God is abundance so that we may serve Him with joy and gladness of heart.

IT HAD TO BE SO

This understanding—that material blessings result from obedience and material curses result from disobedience—was brought home to me personally in a way I will never forget. I was preaching in New Zealand on God's financial provision for His people, and I had prepared an outline that I was following as I preached. But, inwardly—in my mind—I was seeing something I had never seen before: a mental picture of Jesus on the cross, atoning for our sins.

As I unfolded the full extent of the poverty curse—hunger, thirst, nakedness. and the lack of all things—it was as if the Holy Spirit was showing me that as Jesus hung on that tree, every one of those four conditions that make up total poverty was being fulfilled. Jesus was hungry; He had not eaten for nearly twenty-four hours. He was thirsty; one of His last utterances on the cross was, "I thirst!" (John 19:28 NKJV). He was naked—and let no pretty religious pictures ever deceive you about that. Scripture states that the soldiers who carried out the execution stripped Him of all His clothes and then divided those items among themselves. (See, for example, Matthew 27:35.) Jesus was in lack of all things. Finally, He was buried in a borrowed burial robe, and He was laid in a borrowed tomb. (See, for example, Matthew 27:57–60.) Literally, Jesus had absolutely nothing.

As I continued to teach, although I was still following my outline, the Holy Spirit was simultaneously showing me more. He revealed to me why Jesus was hungry, why He was thirsty, why He was naked, and why He lacked all things. The reason? *It had to be so in order for Him to exhaust the poverty curse on our behalf.* Jesus took the complete curse away once and for all so that you and I, as redeemed believers through the blood of Jesus, might not need to endure the iron yoke of the poverty curse. We can thank God that even though all of us have been disobedient, Jesus took upon Himself the iniquity of us all. Our rebellion and all its evil consequences—including poverty—were visited upon Jesus as He hung on the cross.

ALWAYS ABOUNDING

This complete exchange is clearly summed up by Paul in the eighth and ninth chapters of 2 Corinthians, where we see the two aspects of the exchange in the material realm. Paul writes about the first aspect in 2 Corinthians 8:9:

> *For you know the grace of our Lord Jesus Christ, that though He was rich, yet for your sake He became poor, that you through His poverty might become rich.* (NASB)

It is very clear that in this exchange, Jesus took our poverty on the cross so we, in turn, might have access to His wealth and abundance through grace. Grace comes solely through Jesus Christ, and it cannot be earned. Grace is appropriated only by faith—and that is our pathway to overcoming the poverty curse and receiving the blessing instead.

The second aspect is further stated by Paul in 2 Corinthians 9:8:

And God is able to make all grace abound to you, that always having all sufficiency in everything, you may have an abundance for every good deed. (NASB)

In the original Greek, this statement is amazing. The word translated *"abound"* and *"abundance"* occurs twice; and the word, or its derivation, rendered *"all,"* *"always,"* *"everything,"* and *"every"* occurs five times in this one verse. It clearly expresses what Jesus has obtained for us. He exhausted the poverty curse so we might inherit the blessings.

The blessings in all three areas—the spiritual, the physical, and the material—have been obtained for us by Jesus Christ. They are summed up in this beautiful verse:

Beloved, I pray that in all respects you may prosper [the material] *and be in good health* [the physical], *just as your soul prospers* [the spiritual]. (3 John 2 NASB)

That is the will of God for you. That is your inheritance! Before you continue reading, why not stop for a moment and thank God for your inheritance? Let's do so together with the following prayer:

Lord, I want to take a moment now to give You my thanks. Thank You, Jesus, that because of Your willingness to go to the cross in my place, all the evil that was due to me was taken by You instead. I am profoundly grateful to You.

Because of what You did on Calvary, all the wealth of the kingdom of God has been made available to me. Instead of abject poverty, I stand to receive incredible riches—both natural and spiritual. Help me to understand this truth more clearly, and to walk in its reality in a way that glorifies You. Amen.

Knowing we have an inheritance and being thankful for it are only the first steps. For the rest of this book, we will search the Scriptures to understand the means by which we may enter into and enjoy all the benefits that Jesus has made available to us.

INHERITING THE BLESSINGS

For you know the grace of our Lord Jesus Christ, that though He was rich, yet for your sake He became poor, that you through His poverty might become rich.

(2 Corinthians 8:9 NASB)

And God is able to make all grace abound to you, that always having all sufficiency in everything, you may have an abundance for every good deed.   (2 Corinthians 9:8 NASB)

6

THE GREATEST BLESSING

You and I are heirs to a kingdom. The New Testament reveals to us that a tremendous inheritance has been made available to us through the death of Jesus on our behalf. It is the purpose of this book to help you, a rightful heir, discover what that inheritance is and how to claim it.

So far, we have established the foundation for our inheritance—the exchange at Calvary. The basic principle that Scripture reveals through the Holy Spirit is this: When Jesus hung on the cross, He was visibly and demonstrably presented as bearing a curse. He did not bear the curse for Himself but for us. On the cross, Jesus took upon Himself the curses due to our disobedience so that, in turn, He might make available to us the blessings due to His obedience.

He was our Substitute! Our Kinsman-Redeemer! The One who took our nature so He might take our place! The result is that through our faith in Him, all these spiritual, physical, and material blessings have been opened to us.

Why is it so important to fully recognize this exchange? Because it is essential to understanding the cross—and the cross is the key to applying the whole message of the gospel to our lives. We must understand this and other spiritual truths in order to claim all the blessings Jesus has provided for us, thus empowering us to enter into our full inheritance. With all this in mind, in this chapter, we will focus on one specific blessing that is singled out among all others.

THE BLESSING OF ABRAHAM

We return to Galatians 3:13–14, the central Scripture passage that speaks about redemption and deliverance from the curse of the Law:

> *Christ redeemed us from the curse of the Law, having become a curse for us—for it is written, "Cursed is everyone who hangs on a tree"—in order that in Christ Jesus the blessing of Abraham might come to the Gentiles, so that we might receive the promise of the Spirit through faith.*
> (Galatians 3:13–14 NASB)

At this point, I would like to focus on a specific reference Paul makes in the above passage. He says, *"In order that in Christ Jesus the blessing of Abraham might come to the Gentiles."* What does the blessing of Abraham have to do with claiming our inheritance?

Paul explains that through our faith in Jesus, who is the Seed of Abraham (see Galatians 3:16), we can be reckoned as the descendants of Abraham, even though we are not Jewish by natural descent (see verse 29). Why? Because Jesus, through His death on the cross, has redeemed God's people from the curse of the broken Law. And now, because of His sacrifice, not only the Jewish people, but also all of us who are Gentiles, are included in the inheritance of Abraham. We have become coheirs of the blessings God promised to Abraham and his descendants.

Accordingly, we need to know exactly what is covered by the blessing of Abraham, which has been opened to us. The answer to this inquiry is very clearly stated in Scripture:

> Now Abraham was old, advanced in age; and the LORD had blessed Abraham in every way.   (Genesis 24:1 NASB)

In other Bible translations, the last part of this verse reads *"in everything"* or *"in all things."* The blessing of Abraham is a very beautiful blessing because it is *in every way, in everything,* and *in all things!* It covers every area of our lives. Nothing is omitted from the blessing of Abraham. We have already seen that the blessings cover three main areas: spiritual, physical, and material—that is *in everything!*

THE PROMISE OF THE FATHER

Yet, in Galatians 3:14, Paul set apart one specific blessing among all the others when he wrote, *"…so that we might receive the promise of the Spirit through faith"* (NASB). In this verse, the word *"Spirit"* has a capital *S* because it is a title of the Holy Spirit. Of all the promises and blessings made available to us through our faith in Jesus, the promise and blessing of the Spirit is singled out above the rest. Jesus spoke of the coming of the Holy Spirit as *"the promise of My Father"* (Luke 24:49 NASB). The Holy Spirit is the specific, special promise of God the Father to every person who becomes His child through faith in Jesus Christ.

The promise of the Spirit is singled out because the Holy Spirit is the key to—and the source of—all the other blessings. *Unless we receive the Holy Spirit, we are not qualified—neither are we able—to enter into our inheritance.* The Holy Spirit is the One who administers the inheritance and makes it available to us.

OUR HELPER

John 14:15–18 records a portion of Jesus's instructions to His disciples when He is about to leave them. Knowing that He will be arrested, die on the cross, be resurrected, and ascend to heaven not long afterward, He tells them:

> *If you love Me, you will keep My commandments. And I will ask the Father, and He will give you another Helper, that He may be with you forever; that is the Spirit of truth, whom the world cannot receive, because it does not behold Him or know Him, but you know Him because He abides with you, and will be in you. I will not leave you as orphans; I will come to you.* (John 14:15–18 NASB)

In this passage, Jesus reassures His disciples, saying, "Since I am going away, I am sending somebody else who will take My place and stay with you. I have only been with you for a brief three-and-a-half years. But another One is coming in My place, and He will never leave you. He will be with you forever."

Who was that "other One" whom the Father would send? He was the Holy Spirit. Jesus calls Him *"the Spirit of truth"* and gives Him a special title: the *"Helper"* (or, in the King James Version, the *"Comforter"*). Without the Holy Spirit, the disciples would have been left as orphans—little children without anybody to help them, advise them, or stand by them. There would have been no one to show them how they could gain their inheritance, which Jesus had bequeathed to them through His death on the cross. Thus, when the Holy Spirit comes to us, He does so as our Helper, and He shows us how we can claim and enter into the inheritance Jesus purchased for us at Calvary.

HOW DOES THE SPIRIT HELP US?

What are some of the specific ways in which the Holy Spirit helps us? In John 14:26, Jesus says to His disciples,

But the Helper, the Holy Spirit, whom the Father will send in My name, He will teach you all things, and bring to your remembrance all that I said to you.   (NASB)

This verse reveals the first two ways in which the Holy Spirit ministers to us as followers of Jesus. First, He teaches us all we need to know of Scripture and divine revelation. Second, He brings to our remembrance all that Jesus taught, which we might otherwise forget. One reason I have confidence in the absolute accuracy of the New Testament record is that I do not believe it depends on human thought or memory. I believe those who wrote the New Testament were taught by the Holy Spirit—and He brought to their remembrance the truths they needed to recollect.

In John 16:13–14, Jesus continues:

But when He, the Spirit of truth, comes, He will guide you into all the truth; for He will not speak on His own initiative, but whatever He hears, He will speak; and He will disclose to you what is to come. He shall glorify Me; for He shall take of Mine, and shall disclose it to you.   (NASB)

Notice, Jesus emphasizes that the Holy Spirit is a Person, not just an influence. He calls Him *"He,"* not *"it."* In these verses, Jesus indicates three additional ministries the Holy Spirit fulfills in our lives when He comes as our Helper. The third way He ministers to us is by guiding us into *"all the truth"* and into the entire knowledge of everything God has for us in Jesus Christ. He is our Guide who leads us into a land through which we could not otherwise find our way—the land of God's promises! The land of our inheritance!

Fourth, Jesus says, *"He will disclose to you what is to come."* The Helper takes away the veil that covers the times that lie ahead, and reveals to us those aspects of the future we need to know. I believe, as the Bible indicates, that we are living in *"perilous times"* (2 Timothy 3:1 NKJV, KJV). This is an age in which tremendous dangers are going to sweep across the face of the earth. We are going to be confronted with challenges and opposition beyond anything previous generations have seen.

We must be prepared. For our safety, we have to rely on the Holy Spirit revealing to us what we need to know about the future. His warnings will enable us to avoid Satan's dangers, pitfalls, and snares, and safely come through the experiences that lie ahead of us. I do not believe this provision is a luxury; I believe it is a necessity. The Holy Spirit will reveal to us the challenges that are to come.

Note that Jesus also says the Holy Spirit will glorify Him. Please remember that the Holy Spirit never comes to glorify Himself or to talk about Himself. His purpose is always to glorify Jesus. The Holy Spirit reveals to us on earth what He Himself has heard in heaven. *"Whatever He hears, He will speak"* (John 16:13 NASB).

Fifth, after saying, *"He shall glorify Me,"* Jesus declares, *"He shall take of Mine, and shall disclose it to you"* (verse 14 NASB). In other words, the Holy Spirit takes all that rightfully belongs to Jesus, which is our inheritance, and discloses it to us. It is therefore only through the Holy Spirit that we come to know our inheritance in Christ.

OUR ADVOCATE

In conclusion, there is one key word that summarizes for us the person of the Holy Spirit, and that word is *advocate*. The same Greek word that is translated as *"Helper"* in John 14:26, *Parakletos*, is translated as *"Advocate"* in 1 John 2:1 (NASB, NKJV), where it is used in reference to Jesus. This sense of the word applies also to the role of the Holy Spirit.

The Holy Spirit comes as our Advocate. *Advocate* is a legal word that defines the role of an attorney. The Holy Spirit is heaven's best lawyer, sent to us so we will not be orphans. He will interpret to us our inheritance in Christ and show us the conditions we must fulfill to enter into that inheritance. He is our Teacher, our Helper, our Comforter, our Advocate, and our Attorney.

In the Old Testament, there is a vivid and beautiful picture of how the Holy Spirit works to bring us into our inheritance with Jesus. This portrayal helps us to know how we must respond to the Spirit in order to enter into all God has promised to us. The picture is framed within a love story, which we will discover in the next chapter of this book.

INHERITING THE BLESSINGS

Christ redeemed us from the curse of the Law, having become a curse for us—for it is written, "Cursed is everyone who hangs on a tree"—in order that in Christ Jesus the blessing of Abraham might come to the Gentiles, so that we might receive the promise of the Spirit through faith.

(Galatians 3:13–14 NASB)

But when He, the Spirit of truth, comes, He will guide you into all the truth; for He will not speak on His own initiative, but whatever He hears, He will speak; and He will disclose to you what is to come. He shall glorify Me; for He shall take of Mine, and shall disclose it to you.   (John 16:13–14 NASB)

7

THE HOLY SPIRIT: OUR SERVANT-GUIDE

God has provided a special Helper and Guide to stand by us and assist us in claiming our inheritance. This special Helper is the Holy Spirit. He is our Advocate who is sent to interpret for us the full extent of our inheritance and to show us the conditions we must meet in order to claim and sustain it.

In connection to this truth, we have identified five specific ways in which the Holy Spirit helps us:

+ He teaches us.

+ He brings to our remembrance things we otherwise could not remember accurately.

+ He guides us into all truth.

+ He discloses what is to come.

+ He discloses to us all that belongs to Christ and therefore to us because we share the inheritance with Christ.

SEEKING A BRIDE

We will now examine more closely the part the Holy Spirit plays in bringing us into our inheritance in Christ. To illustrate this vital role of the Spirit, we are going to look at that vivid and beautiful picture from the Old Testament I referred to at the end of the last chapter. In Genesis 24, we find the story of how Abraham obtained a bride for his son Isaac. It is a story of events that actually took place. But it is also a parable acted out in history that reveals spiritual truths—truths that are especially important to us as believers in Jesus today.

At the time this story takes place, Abraham was settled in Canaan, the land God had promised to him. He and his wife, Sarah, had finally received their miracle son, Isaac, who was to be the heir of all that God intended to provide for His people. Isaac had grown to adulthood, and Abraham wanted to find a wife for him, but he did not want his son to take a wife from the daughters of the Canaanites who lived in the land. Therefore, he assigned the task of finding an appropriate wife for his son to his senior servant, the main steward of his house. Abraham told this servant to go back to Mesopotamia, the country of Abraham's origin, and find a bride from among his own relatives who were still living there.

The servant equipped himself with ten camels laden with valuable gifts and set out for Mesopotamia. On the way, he prayed that the Lord would direct him to the young woman who was His choice to be the bride for Isaac. When the servant arrived in Mesopotamia, he stopped at a well and prayed a very specific prayer. His plan was that when the right woman came along, he would ask her to give him a drink. If she responded by not merely giving him water but also drawing water from the well for all his camels, that would be the sign. He would know she was the woman chosen to be Isaac's bride. (See Genesis 24:1–14.)

AN ANSWERED PRAYER

When the servant had finished praying, along came Rebekah, who was a member of the same clan as Abraham. She arrived at the well with her water jar, and when the servant asked her for a drink, she not only gave him water but immediately, of her own initiative, proceeded to draw water for his camels. Why is this of such major significance? Because the servant had ten camels, and they had made a long journey through a desert. It has been estimated that a thirsty camel can drink up to forty gallons of water. Therefore, if Rebekah was able to draw water for ten camels, that meant she was an active, vigorous woman. How so? She had to draw about four hundred gallons of water out of a well—with a bucket!

After that, the servant brought out the beautiful gifts he was carrying. When he gave them to Rebekah, she immediately adorned herself with them. Her next step was to introduce Abraham's steward to her family. The family welcomed the servant into their home, even making provision for his camels. At the family gathering, Abraham's steward made the presentation concerning the destiny God had for Rebekah as the wife of Isaac. To this proposal, Rebekah responded in faith and agreed to go with the servant. Her family blessed her, and she set out with the steward to take the long journey back to meet the man she was due to marry. Bear in mind, she had never seen Abraham or Isaac. Her only contact with the family into which she was going to marry was through the servant. (See Genesis 24:15–61.)

THE UNNAMED SERVANT

This beautiful story involving Abraham, Sarah, Isaac, the steward, and Rebekah is actually a parable of God the Father finding a bride for His only Son, Jesus Christ. In this interpretation, Abraham, the father of Isaac, represents God the Father. Isaac, the only son, represents God the Son. Rebekah, the chosen bride, represents the church, Christ's chosen bride.

But there is one more major character in this story—the unnamed servant. I see in the Scripture's depiction of this unnamed servant a self-portrait of the Holy Spirit. Perhaps it is the clearest portrait in all of Scripture regarding who the Holy Spirit really is and what He does. It always blesses me that the Holy Spirit, like the unnamed servant, is so modest and unassuming He never even gives Himself a name. The term referring to His role in the allegory is simply "the servant."

THE HOLY SPIRIT'S ROLE

SEVEN FACTS ABOUT THE SERVANT

As we compare the role of Abraham's steward to that of the Holy Spirit, we will begin by observing seven significant facts about the servant's relationship to Abraham, Isaac, and Rebekah.

First, it is stated very clearly that the servant had charge of all that Abraham owned; he was in complete control of the entire inheritance.

Second, he sought nothing for himself, but only for Abraham and Isaac.

Third, it was his responsibility to find a bride for Isaac.

Fourth, he came with ten camels bearing gifts.

Fifth, he confronted Rebekah with the choice that settled her destiny.

Sixth, he was Rebekah's only source of information concerning Abraham and Isaac.

Seventh, it was he who guided Rebekah to her bridegroom.

SEVEN TRUTHS ABOUT THE HOLY SPIRIT

Let's apply the above seven facts about the servant to seven truths about the Holy Spirit in relation to the church.

First, the Holy Spirit is the Administrator of the total inheritance of Christ. He is the One who possesses the riches of Christ, reveals them, and imparts them to us.

Second, the Holy Spirit seeks nothing for Himself. His aim is to glorify the Father and the Son.

Third, it is the responsibility of the Holy Spirit in the world to "find" the bride, the church, for the Son of God, Jesus Christ.

Fourth, when the Holy Spirit comes into our lives, He comes with many beautiful and wonderful gifts.

Fifth, He is the One who presents to us the choice concerning Jesus—and our decision settles our destiny for time and eternity.

Sixth, He is our only Source of direct information concerning God the Father and God the Son. We cannot see the other persons of the Godhead—the Holy Spirit (though Himself unseen) must reveal them to us.

Seventh, He is the One who guides us through this world and leads us to our wedding with our heavenly Bridegroom.

THE CHURCH'S RESPONSE

SEVEN FACTS ABOUT REBEKAH

Having seen how the servant of Abraham is a picture of the Holy Spirit in His relationship to the bride of Christ, we will now look at the story from another point of view. We will examine how Rebekah is a picture of the church. She exemplifies the response the church must make to the Holy Spirit in order to qualify to be the bride of Christ. To clarify this illustration, I will point out seven facts about Rebekah's response and its significance for us as believers in Jesus.

First, her initial contact was with the servant—not with Abraham or Isaac.

Second, her response to the servant determined her destiny.

Third, her immediate response was to serve Abraham's steward. She began to draw water for his camels, which was very hard work.

Fourth, she received the gifts the servant brought.

Fifth, she adorned herself with those gifts, and they visibly marked her as the chosen bride.

Sixth, she made room in her home for the servant and his camels—and camels take up a lot of room!

Seventh, she followed the servant in faith to her destination and her destiny.

SEVEN TRUTHS ABOUT THE CHURCH

How does Rebekah's example typify the ways in which we, as the church, are required to respond to the Holy Spirit?

First, our initial contact with God is always through His Holy Spirit. He is the One who first reaches into our lives and begins to reveal the Father and the Son to us.

Second, our response to the Holy Spirit determines our destiny for time and eternity. In the story, the point of decision presented to Rebekah through the servant signified a choice that would settle her destiny for the rest of her life. When she said yes to the servant, her destiny was in accordance with the will of God and was good. But if she had said no to the servant, the rest of her destiny would never have been revealed to her. She would have missed all that God had purposed for her life.

Third, our Christianity must be characterized by active faith—faith with works. Rebekah drawing the water from the well is a good picture of what that means. Her response was to serve

Abraham's steward. I call that response "faith with works." She did not just believe. She did not merely say yes. She got busy! She dipped her bucket down into that well and drew about four hundred gallons of water for the camels.

Fourth, we must accept the gifts the Spirit offers us, just as Rebekah accepted the gifts the servant brought her. We cannot accept someone while rejecting the gifts that he or she offers. For example, if a young man saves up to buy a beautiful engagement ring for the young woman he wants to marry, the young woman cannot refuse the ring and still marry the man. Accepting or rejecting the ring is an indication of her attitude toward him. It is the same with us in our relationship with the Holy Spirit. We cannot reject the Holy Spirit's gifts and expect to be part of the bride of Christ.

Fifth, when the gifts of the Holy Spirit come into operation in the church, the church is visibly set apart as the bride of Christ, just as the gifts from the servant visibly marked Rebekah as the chosen bride.

Sixth, receiving the Holy Spirit into our lives may call for many changes. We may need to clear out space in our lives to make room for what God wants—similar to the way Rebekah made room in her home for the servant and his camels. Radical changes may be required as we put the will of God ahead of our own convenience and comfort.

Seventh, the only way to safely journey through this world and finally arrive at the ultimate encounter with our heavenly Bridegroom is by following the Holy Spirit. Rebekah followed the servant to her appointed destination, and we must likewise allow the Spirit to lead us to our true home.

In closing, I want to emphasize that Rebekah's relationship to the servant was essential to her destiny in God. This is equally true for us as believers in Jesus Christ—our relationship to the Holy

Spirit will determine the outcome of our lives. If we snub the Holy Spirit, we cannot enter into our destiny. He is the Helper—sent to enable us to discover and receive our full inheritance.

INHERITING THE BLESSINGS

Christ also loved the church and gave Himself up for her; that He might sanctify her, having cleansed her by the washing of water with the word, that He might present to Himself the church in all her glory, having no spot or wrinkle or any such thing; but that she should be holy and blameless.
(Ephesians 5:25–27 NASB)

"Let us rejoice and be glad and give the glory to Him, for the marriage of the Lamb has come and His bride has made herself ready." And it was given to her to clothe herself in fine linen, bright and clean; for the fine linen is the righteous acts of the saints.
(Revelation 19:7–8 NASB)

PART TWO:

GREAT AND PRECIOUS PROMISES

8

PROVISION
IN THE PROMISES

The Holy Spirit has a special role in enabling us to obtain our inheritance. He is our Helper sent from heaven. He is our Advocate—our Attorney—able to interpret for us the full extent of our inheritance, along with the conditions we must meet for our claim to be substantiated. He is also our Servant-Guide, fulfilling the same role in relation to the church that Abraham's servant played in relation to Rebekah. The Holy Spirit presents the choice that determines our destiny. When we say yes to Him, He equips us with His gifts, reveals to us the Father and the Son, and guides us to our heavenly Bridegroom. In these and so many other ways, we depend on God's Holy Spirit.

In part two of this book, we will explore the parameters through which our inheritance comes to us. These parameters are very important—yet they involve truths many Christians have never clearly understood. Consequently, they have not been able to enter fully into the inheritance God intends for them.

GOD IS THE ONLY SOURCE; JESUS IS THE ONLY CHANNEL

To begin, we will look at a key passage for understanding our inheritance:

> *Grace and peace be yours in abundance through the knowledge of God and of Jesus our Lord. His divine power* [God's power] *has given us everything we need for life and godliness through our knowledge of Him who called us by His own glory and goodness. Through these* [the glory and goodness of Jesus] *He* [God] *has given us His very great and precious promises, so that through them* [the promises] *you may participate in* ["*become partakers of*" NASB] *the divine nature and escape the corruption in the world caused by evil desires.*
>
> (2 Peter 1:2–4 NIV)

I marvel at the writings of Peter! He was a comparatively unlearned man—yet he conveys so many tremendous truths and concepts, with wording that indicates a high level of education. How was that possible? Peter received his education through the Holy Spirit—the best Educator in the world!

In the above passage, we can identify four important points that follow a logical order. Verse 2 begins, *"Grace and peace be yours in abundance...."* Thus, the first point is that God's provision for us is abundant. God is not a stingy God. Neither is He in financial or spiritual need, making Him unable to give to us. God is the Author and Source of everything in the universe. When He provides for His people, He provides in abundance.

Peter continues, *"...through the knowledge of God and of Jesus our Lord"* (verse 2). This phrase indicates that all of God's provisions come through knowing God the Father and Jesus the Son. There is no other way for divine provision to come to us. I like to express it this way: *God is the only Source; Jesus is the only Channel.* I always emphasize the word *only.* God is the *only* Source; Jesus is the *only* Channel.

Peter then makes an astonishing statement at the beginning of verse 3: "[God's] *divine power has* [already] *given us everything we need…*." Let's be very careful to observe the tense of the verb in this statement. It does not say "God *will* give us everything we need"; it says "[God] **has given** us everything we need." God has already supplied all our needs. Please lay hold of this fact because, if you miss it, you will not be able to understand the nature of God's provision.

In the second part of verse 3, Peter returns to the theme of everything being contained in Jesus: "…*through our knowledge of Him who called us by His own glory and goodness.*" Peter obviously considers it so important for us to recognize our entire inheritance is contained in Jesus that he states it twice—in verses 2 and 3. However, although the word *"knowledge"* is used in both of these verses, the Greek meaning of *"knowledge"* is slightly different in verse 3 than in verse 2. In verse 2, it indicates an intellectual or theological knowledge of Jesus. In verse 3, it designates "acknowledging." It signifies seeing who Jesus is, recognizing Him, and giving Him His rightful place in our lives.

I believe it is worthwhile to repeat the four observations from 1 Peter 2:1–4 we have just identified, because they are the basis for all that follows in the rest of this chapter:

1. God's provision for us is abundant.

2. God is the *only* Source; Jesus is the *only* Channel.

3. God's power *has already* given us everything we will ever need. It has all been done; God has already given!

4. Our entire inheritance is contained in knowing Jesus. However, it is not just a matter of knowing Him intellectually or theologically. We need to know Him as a Person and give Him His rightful place in our lives. Really, it means making Jesus Lord in every area of our lives.

"WHY DON'T WE HAVE IT?"

We have just established that God has already given us everything we will ever need. However, you may look at your life at this point and say, "Well, if God has given me everything I need, I don't see it. There are needs in my life that have not been met—even though I am a believer, doing my best to walk the Christian road."

Peter gives us the solution to this problem in verse 4 of our key passage. It is a truth the Holy Spirit revealed to me years ago, and it has been a major factor in my own spiritual progress when facing the inevitable questions, "Where is the very thing God has given? If God has already given it, why don't I see it? Why don't I seem to have it?" We will start by looking at the first part of the verse:

> *Through these* [the glory and goodness of Jesus] *He* [God] *has given us His very great and precious promises....*
> (2 Peter 1:4 NIV)

Previously, we read, "[God] *has given us everything we need*" (verse 3). Now, this verse says, "[God] *has given us His very great and precious promises.*" The conclusion is very simple and logical: *everything we need is contained in the promises of God.* In the promises God has given us, He has provided everything we will require for time and eternity. I like to express it this way: "The provision is in the promises."

This explains why, on the one hand, God says He has given us everything we need—and yet, on the other hand, so many Christians are obviously lacking what they need. They have yet to discover where God's provision is. *God's provision is in His promises.* Thus, in order to receive your provision, you must *know* the promises of God. Then, once you discover those promises, you must know how to possess them.

RECEIVING GOD'S OWN NATURE

I will deal more specifically with the "how to" of possessing the promises in subsequent chapters. For now, let's look at this passage once more and see what happens in our lives when we realize that God's provision is in His promises. When we find the promises we need, and then begin to claim and apply them, some amazing results will follow. Peter says in verse 4,

> ...*so that through them* [the promises] *you may participate in* ["*become partakers of*" NASB] *the divine nature and escape the corruption in the world caused by evil desires.*
>
> (2 Peter 1:4 NIV)

Peter states two results of claiming the promises of God. The first is "positive," and the second is "negative." The positive result is that we participate in the nature of God Himself—which is an amazing statement! If that concept were not included in the Bible, I do not think I would dare to believe it. However, it is explicitly stated that by appropriating God's promises, *we become partakers of His nature.* The very nature of God Himself comes into us. We reflect more and more of His divine character. Let me state that again: when we act on God's promises, appropriating them and making them ours in experience, a transformation occurs: *the very nature of God begins to come into us.*

This positive result logically leads us to the negative result: we "*escape the corruption in the world caused by evil desires.*" Our old fallen nature is corrupt—morally, spiritually, and physically—and it has to be expelled and replaced. The good news is that, as the nature of God comes in, it replaces the corruption with a godly nature that is incorruptible. A new kind of nature, personality, and life comes into us as we appropriate the promises of God. It is the nature, personality, and life of God Himself, coming into us as we believe and act on the promises He has given us in His Word.

Thus, to our first four observations, identified earlier in this chapter, we can add these three points:

5. God's provision is in His promises.

6. By appropriating the promises, we participate in the divine nature; the very nature of God Himself comes into us.

7. In proportion to the extent that we take on the nature of God, we *"escape the corruption in the world caused by evil desires,"* because the nature of God and corruption are incompatible.

This entire process leads us to a very important and wonderful conclusion: ultimately, God Himself becomes our inheritance! It is not just a matter of accumulating gifts, blessings, or experiences from God. We become partakers of His very nature.

Beloved, never stop short of God! Don't settle for gifts, blessings, or experiences—as wonderful as they may be. The real purpose of God is that you inherit God Himself through His promises!

INHERITING THE BLESSINGS

His divine power has given us everything we need for life and godliness through our knowledge of Him who called us by His own glory and goodness. Through these He has given us His very great and precious promises, so that through them you may participate in the divine nature and escape the corruption in the world caused by evil desires.   (2 Peter 1:3–4 NIV)

My eyes stay open through the watches of the night, that I may meditate on your promises.   (Psalm 119:148 NIV)

9

THE PROMISES: OUR INHERITANCE

Our study of 2 Peter 1:2–4 has revealed seven truths that relate to God's marvelous provision for us. I would like to restate these truths because they are an essential foundation for this chapter:

1. God's provision is abundant.

2. God is the *only* Source; Jesus is the *only* Channel.

3. God's power has already given us everything we need. It is not something God *is going to do*; it is something He *has already done*.

4. All of our inheritance is contained in knowing, or acknowledging, Jesus; that is, not just knowing about Him intellectually but drawing close to Him and giving Him His rightful place in our lives.

5. God's provision is in His promises. This is the key to understanding everything about our inheritance in Christ.

6. By appropriating the promises, we participate in the divine nature; the very nature of God Himself comes into us.

7. In proportion to the extent that we take on the nature of God, we *"escape the corruption in the world caused by evil desires"* (2 Peter 1:4 NIV). The nature of God and corruption are incompatible. Wherever God's nature imprints our lives, there is no more room for corruption.

A PATTERN FOR ENTERING OUR INHERITANCE

Now we will delve deeper into how we are to appropriate God's promises. The Old Testament book of Joshua describes how God's people, the Israelites, entered into the inheritance God had promised for them. Rightly understood, this account provides a pattern we can follow as we enter into the inheritance Jesus has won for us.

At the very beginning of the first chapter of Joshua, we find some important points that are essential for understanding what follows in the rest of the book.

> *Now it came about after the death of Moses the servant of the LORD that the LORD spoke to Joshua the son of Nun, Moses' servant, saying, "Moses My servant is dead; now therefore arise, cross this Jordan, you and all this people, to the land which I am giving to them, to the sons of Israel. Every place on which the sole of your foot treads, I have given it to you, just as I spoke to Moses."* (Joshua 1:1–3 NASB)

The Lord begins His conversation with Joshua by stating, *"Moses my servant is dead; now therefore...."* This declaration points to a particular principle of the spiritual life: often a "death" must precede a new work of God. Moses had been one of the greatest leaders God ever gave to His people. Yet it was only after his death that the Israelites could move into their inheritance. Although they mourned Moses's death, his absence was not a disaster—rather, it was a necessary preface to their next steps into their inheritance.

We may well find this principle at work in our own spiritual journeys. Frequently, something in us—or in a work God has previously done—must "die" before we can step into the next move He has prepared for us. In my own life, I have often observed that when God is leading me into something new, something old must first be released. Our spiritual journeys may be compared to the cycle of the seasons. At the end of the summer comes fall. Then winter arrives, which is a time of death. But out of that time of death, there emerges the newness and renewal of spring.

The second point from this passage is that God required *all* the people to cross over the Jordan. This is so different from the contemporary church—if we get a 50 percent response from the people, we think we are doing pretty well. However, in the matter of His people entering the promised land, God said not one of them was to be left behind; they were all to cross over.

By crossing over, however, they had to let go of the old life they knew. I believe there will be a time like that for the people of God. All who want to belong to God's family and move into what He has for them are going to have to leave something behind in order to cross over into their inheritance.

LEGAL VERSUS EXPERIENTIAL

Please note the verb tenses God uses in the above passage from Joshua 1. In verse 2, He uses the present tense: "*the land which I am giving.*" But in verse 3, He uses the perfect tense: "*I have given it to you.*" Here is the lesson: Once God says, "I give it to you," He does not need to give it again. After that, as far as God is concerned, it has been given. It is a settled matter. Once it has been given, it has been given!

Thus, for the Israelites, from that point onward, the legal right to the entire land had been given to them by God. Yet *they still did not have experiential possession of it.* They did not own any more of the land experientially than they did before God made His declaration. Likewise, there is a vast difference between the *legal right* and the *experiential possession* of what God has promised us. This is extremely important for every believer in Jesus Christ to understand.

I have sometimes commented that if the Israelites had been like some Christians today, after God said, "I've given you the whole land," they would have lined up along the east bank of the Jordan River, looked westward across the river into the land, and said, "It's all ours!" That would have been true in a legal sense. But it would not have been true experientially because the Canaanites still dominated the land. As we appropriate God's promises, we need to bear in mind this core principle from the book of Joshua: *It is one thing to have the legal right; it is another thing to have the experiential possession.*

THE PROMISED LAND—AND A LAND OF PROMISES

What was the actual process by which Israel moved into the land? Their first two successes came through miracles. A miracle opened the way for them to cross the Jordan River. (See Joshua 3.) Then, through another miracle, they captured the first city, Jericho. (See Joshua 6.) After these two incidents, however, they had to fight for the rest of their inheritance in the land.

In fact, the only way they actually gained experiential possession of the land was by placing their feet on the ground they were claiming. God said to them, in effect, "Every place where you set the sole of your foot will be yours in experience—not just in legal right." (See Joshua 1:3.)

The Israelites' entire experience of stepping into their inheritance is a clear and practical example for us as we receive our own inheritance in Christ. The Hebrew name *Joshua* is the same in the original language as the name *Jesus*. They are two different forms of the same name. Comparing the two inheritances, here is the conclusion we can make: In the Old Testament, under a leader named Joshua, God led His people into the promised land as their inheritance. In the New Testament, under a leader named Jesus, God leads His people into *a land of promises* as their inheritance.

From the time we are born again and become God's children legally, we are heirs to all that God has for us. This is what Paul says in the eighth chapter of Romans:

> *The Spirit Himself* [Holy Spirit] *testifies with our spirit that we are God's children.*   (Romans 8:16 NIV)

The witness of the Holy Spirit is essential to our inheritance. We must know, through the witness of God's Spirit, that we really are the children of God. Otherwise, our claim to be His children is not endorsed by the Holy Spirit, and this is something that must be a reality for us. Paul goes on to say:

> *Now if we are children, then we are heirs—heirs of God and co-heirs with Christ....*   (Romans 8:17 NIV)

This is exciting! The entire inheritance of God belongs to us because we share that inheritance with Jesus Christ. Everything that belongs to Jesus Christ belongs likewise to us as sons and daughters of God. However, there is another "*if*" that follows— and sometimes people read the Bible and skip the "if's." This is a very important "if," and we need to note it:

> *Now if we are children, then we are heirs—heirs of God and co-heirs with Christ,* **if** *indeed we share in His sufferings in order that we may also share in His glory.*
>   (Romans 8:17 NIV)

We are heirs to the whole inheritance of God, with its blessings. But we are also heirs to Christ's sufferings. We cannot skip the sufferings and expect to inherit the blessings. That is very clear. The condition is "if we suffer with Him."

PRINCIPLES FOR POSSESSING OUR INHERITANCE

How do we gain experiential possession of our inheritance as Christians? It is not enough merely to line up on the east bank of the river and look across at our inheritance and say, "I've got it all!" So often, people "have it all" in theory or doctrine, but they do not "have it all" in real experience. I have actually met people who told me, "I got it all when I accepted Jesus." Here is my answer to that statement: "You got it all legally, but you didn't necessarily get it all experientially." That is exactly what is illustrated by the history of Israel. Sometimes I will add, "Well, if you've got it all, where is it? Let's see it! Demonstrate it! Use it! Let's have the evidence."

If we lack experiential possession of God's promises, we need to apply the lesson of Joshua and the Israelites. What are the principles that apply to us? I would suggest three main principles for experiential possession of our inheritance.

First, where necessary, God will do miracles. But God may not do miracles where they are not necessary.

Second, like Israel, most of our inheritance will come through "fighting" for it. We will not enter into our inheritance unless we are prepared to take on the powers of darkness that oppose us. We will have to defeat them with the spiritual weapons God has made available to us. Let me say this: *Christians who will not fight will not enter their inheritance.*

There is a little word used in common speech today that applies to our need to fight for our inheritance—it is the word *guts*. Some people might consider this term to be rather vulgar; they would prefer the expression "intestinal fortitude." Whichever way you wish to express it, I want to suggest that you will need "guts." You can probably come into much of your inheritance without a lot of theological knowledge, but I doubt whether you will get much of it without guts. It takes guts to be a Christian. It takes guts to enter our inheritance!

The third principle from the experience of Joshua and the Israelites is this: We must set our feet on what God has promised us. We must take possession of it for ourselves, individually and personally—and this is where suffering comes in. When we begin to fight for our inheritance, we will find that we inevitably share in Christ's sufferings.

Accordingly, we have two responsibilities in claiming our inheritance in Christ:

1. We must be prepared to fight.

2. We must set our feet on what we claim to be our inheritance.

Therefore: *Fight! Set your feet!*

Would you like to make these your declarations concerning your pursuit of God's inheritance? Why not speak them out now? Are you ready?

I will fight!

I will set my feet on my inheritance in God!

I'm glad you have made those proclamations. And I say amen to them!

INHERITING THE BLESSINGS

Moses My servant is dead; now therefore arise, cross this Jordan, you and all this people, to the land which I am giving to them, to the sons of Israel. Every place on which the sole of your foot treads, I have given it to you, just as I spoke to Moses.   (Joshua 1:2–3 NASB)

Now if we are children, then we are heirs—heirs of God and co-heirs with Christ, if indeed we share in His sufferings in order that we may also share in His glory.

(Romans 8:17 NIV)

10

PROMISES AVAILABLE
TO US

The example of the Israelites entering into their inheritance, led by Joshua, provides a wonderful pattern for us as Christians entering our inheritance in Christ. We have summarized the parallel between the two inheritances in this way: In the Old Testament, under a leader named Joshua, God led His people into *the promised land*. In the New Testament, under a leader named Jesus, God leads His people into *a land of promises*.

ALL THE PROMISES

What is this land of promises? Simply stated, it is the full extent of our inheritance, which is no less than all the promises of God. The key verse that unfolds this truth to us is 2 Corinthians 1:20. There are different ways of rendering this verse because, in the original language of the New Testament, the Greek is so condensed it is hard to translate. I will quote from two Bible versions: the King James Version, which is worded very beautifully, and the *New International Version*, which also provides a powerful translation of this particular verse.

For all the promises of God in Him [Jesus Christ] *are yea,*
and in Him Amen, unto the glory of God by us.

(2 Corinthians 1:20 KJV)

For no matter how many promises God has made, they are
"Yes" in Christ. And so through Him the "Amen" is spoken by
us to the glory of God.   (2 Corinthians 1:20 NIV)

"YES" AND "AMEN"

Whichever translation of 2 Corinthians 1:20 we prefer, certain very important points emerge from it. First, Paul writes of
"all" (KJV) the promises. The inheritance is *all* the promises of
God. *All* God's promises are available to us. Not some of them,
but all of them.

Second, in this verse, the verb is in the present tense. "All the
promises of God *are* 'Yes' and 'Amen.'" The promises are not in
the past, nor are they in the future. In contemporary Christianity,
some people have an unfortunate way of interpreting Scripture
that robs them, in their present experience, of practically everything that is worth having. They believe miracles were for the
past—for the era of Jesus's ministry and the early church. They
believe prosperity and healing are for the future—for the coming
millennium. In the meantime, they are left with a mere crust that
just barely sustains life.

However, that is not what this Scripture tells us. Speaking of
God's promises, it does not say they "were." It does not say they
"will be." It says they *are now*. Our inheritance is right now—and
it is all the promises of God.

The verse also clearly says that the *"promises...are 'Yes' in*
Christ" (NIV). We have seen that there is only one Source, God;
and there is only one Channel, Jesus. There is no other way that
these promises can come to us except from God through Jesus.

Paul states that the promises are "*Yes.*" That is very emphatic! It is one of the most emphatic and positive statements in the entire Bible.

God doesn't say, "I'll do this," but then retract His offer when you ask Him for it, replying, "Well, as a matter of fact, I'm not sure I will do it after all." Instead, He says, "I promised it. I meant it. And I'll stand behind what I promised." All His promises are "*Yes.*"

You may not realize, however, that we must add something to God's "*Yes.*" The *New International Version* says, "*Through Him* [Jesus] *the 'Amen' is spoken by us to the glory of God.*" This is a vivid picture. If you find a promise, you can ask, "God, did You mean this?" And God will answer, "Yes, I meant it." His answer is "*Yes,*" but in order to appropriate the promise, we must respond to God's "*Yes*" with our "*Amen.*" The word *amen* means "so let it be" or "be it established." It is our "Amen" that makes a promise ours at a given moment and in a given situation.

The next exciting statement is that all this is "*by us.*" I am so glad for those two words! "*Us*" means ordinary people just like you and me. Paul does not say "by the apostles," "by great preachers," or "by evangelists." He says "*by us.*" All God's promises are available to us—here and now.

TO THE GLORY OF GOD

The final point we need to see is that these promises are "*to the glory of God*" (2 Corinthians 1:20 NIV). The ultimate purpose of our existence is to glorify God. The Lord has so arranged the promises He has given to us that every time we appropriate those promises in faith, we glorify Him. And the more we appropriate God's promises, the more we glorify Him!

Thus, when it comes to the promises, there are two alternatives before us: unbelief, which robs God of His glory; or faith, which gives God the glory due to Him. Romans 3:23 says, *"For all have sinned and fall short of the glory of God"* (NASB, NIV). The essential nature of sin and unbelief is that it robs God of the glory He deserves. In contrast, in Romans 4, we see the pattern of Abraham, who is set forth before us as the father of all who believe. (See verse 11.) Paul says this about Abraham:

> *Yet he did not waver through unbelief regarding the promise of God, but was strengthened in his faith and gave glory to God, being fully persuaded that God had power to do what He had promised.* (Romans 4:20–21 NIV)

Please notice Abraham's firm belief. What was his conviction? He believed that if God promised anything, then He had the power to do it. Abraham never wavered in that conviction; He just responded to God's "Yes" with his "Amen"—and in that way, he gave glory to Him. Again, it is unbelief that robs God of the glory due to Him. But when we claim the promises of God with unwavering faith, we give Him the glory He deserves.

EIGHT THOUSAND PROMISES

I find the *New International Version*'s rendering of 2 Corinthians 1:20 very helpful for bringing out a further point. Let us look at that verse once more: **"For no matter how many promises God has made,** they are 'Yes' in Christ. And so through Him the 'Amen' is spoken by us to the glory of God." Someone has calculated that there are about eight thousand promises of God in the Bible. All of these promises are available to us when we need them, even though we do not need them all at the same time.

At any given moment, we may need to put our finger on one particular promise that represents God's provision for our need in that situation. I sum up 2 Corinthians 1:20 like this: "Every promise that fits my situation and meets my need is for me now." It is important to remember, however, that our ultimate objective, in all circumstances, is to glorify God.

Another important factor to keep in mind, which many Christians overlook, is that most of God's promises are conditional! In many cases (but not all), when God gives a promise, He says to His people, "If you will do so-and-so, then I will do so-and-so." When the promise is conditional, we have no right to claim it unless we first meet the condition.

The promises of blessings we looked at in earlier chapters are good examples of this. We saw a significant list of blessings in Deuteronomy 28. Let's bear in mind that the condition stated at the beginning of that chapter is the following: *"If you will diligently* [listen to the voice of] *the* Lord *your God...."* (verse 1 NASB). Logically, if we do not diligently listen to the voice of the Lord, we have no scriptural right to claim those blessings. We must fulfill God's conditions.

In light of this truth, it is essential for us to keep His conditions in mind. The fulfillment of God's promises does not depend upon our circumstances but upon our meeting His conditions. In other words, we must keep our eyes on fulfilling the conditions and not be influenced by our particular situations. Often, when believers find a promise that will answer a need, they begin to claim it. But then they look at their circumstances and find them totally unfavorable. Due to those circumstances, they may conclude, "Well, it's true that God made that promise. But this is not a situation in which God can fulfill it." This is a totally wrong conclusion—and it is the point at which many of us lose out on our inheritance.

WHY DO WE NEED TO WAIT?

To better understand this reality, let's go back to the example of Abraham. God had promised Abraham that a son from his own body would be his heir. (See, for example, Genesis 15:1–6.)

Abraham reached the age of eighty-six, but no son had come. So he tried on his own to see the promise fulfilled through Sarah's maid, Hagar. He produced Ishmael, but Ishmael was not to be the heir. (See Genesis 16–17.) Why did God eventually allow Abraham to get to the age of ninety-nine before He fulfilled His promise? And why does God often allow us to come to a position of seeming impossibility before He fulfills the promises we are claiming? I believe there are at least two practical reasons, among others.

First, when we must wait until we are powerless, we are emptied of all self-confidence. We come to the point where we know that if something is going to be done, God has to be the One to do it. That is the point to which Abraham finally came. He knew his own body was, for the purposes of procreation, dead. He knew that Sarah's womb was dead. He knew that there was no longer any natural possibility for the promise to be fulfilled. Therefore, he had to focus his eyes solely and exclusively on God—because there was no one else who could do it.

Second, I believe God allows us to come to a point of seeming impossibility because, when this happens and He intervenes, all the glory goes to Him. Remember, this is the ultimate purpose of the promises! When there is a possibility we can do something by our own effort, then we may take some of the credit for it. But when we come to the place where we know we cannot do it by our own effort, and all our self-confidence is exhausted, then the glory truly goes to God!

In the next chapter, we are going to take another look at the story of Joshua as he leads the people of God into the promised land. This is an exciting point in our journey because we know that Joshua's leadership is a model for how we are to be led into the land of promises. As we understand more about this pattern and its principles, we will be prepared to appropriate specific and practical promises God has given to us in our inheritance in Jesus.

INHERITING THE BLESSINGS

For all the promises of God in Him [Jesus Christ] *are yea, and in Him Amen, unto the glory of God by us.*

(2 Corinthians 1:20 KJV)

For no matter how many promises God has made, they are "Yes" in Christ. And so through him the "Amen" is spoken by us to the glory of God. (2 Corinthians 1:20 NIV)

Not one of all the LORD's good promises to the house of Israel failed; every one was fulfilled. (Joshua 21:45 NIV)

11

THINK, SPEAK, AND ACT

In this chapter, we are going to consider a promise that, in a certain sense, is the key to claiming all the other promises. But before we do, we must make sure we have firmly grasped two important foundational points.

First, God's entire provision for His people is in His promises! The key Scripture passage supporting this point is 2 Peter 1:3–4:

> His [God's] divine power has given us everything we need for life and godliness through our knowledge of Him who called us by His own glory and goodness. Through these He has given us His very great and precious promises, so that through them you may participate in the divine nature and escape the corruption in the world caused by evil desires. (NIV)

There are two truths in these verses we especially need to grasp. Both of them are stated in the perfect tense, meaning they have already been accomplished. Verse 3 tells us "[God's] *divine power **has given** us everything we need for life and godliness.*" Please notice once again that this verse does not say God *is going* to give us everything we need. It says He *has already* given it to us. Verse 4 further emphasizes this truth, saying, *"He [God] **has given** us His very great and precious promises."* Clearly, God has already given us everything we are ever going to need. But how does it come to us? He provides our inheritance in the form of His promises.

The second foundational point is that God's promises are our inheritance. As we saw previously, in the Old Testament, under a leader named Joshua, God led His people into the promised land. In the New Testament, under a leader named Jesus (the same name as Joshua in the Hebrew form), God leads His people into a land of promises. As we walk through this land of promises, our ultimate goal is to develop a clear view of our inheritance. That way, we can better understand how to possess it.

THE KEY TO ALL PROMISES

Let us now explore the promise that is the key to claiming all the other promises. It is the promise the Lord gave to Joshua when He commissioned him to lead God's people into their inheritance:

This book of the law shall not depart from your mouth, but you shall meditate on it day and night, so that you may be careful to do according to all that is written in it; for then you will make your way prosperous, and then you will have success. (Joshua 1:8 NASB)

This promise gives complete assurance of success: *"Then you will make your way prosperous, and then you will have success."* In fact, two outcomes are combined in this wonderful statement: prosperity and success. As you are reading these words, you might think, "Well, that was Joshua—but I am not Joshua." Even though this is true, please remember that God is *"no respecter of persons"* (Acts 10:34 KJV). That means He has no favorites. If you meet God's conditions when facing the challenges of life, He will do for you exactly what He would have done for Joshua—or for any of

His other great servants. It is not the personality that impresses God; rather, it is the obedience to His conditions.

Thus, we begin with this promise: "*You will make your way prosperous, and…you will have success.*" In my dealings with human beings over many years, I have discovered that nobody really wants to fail! In every person, there resides a deep desire and longing to succeed. I believe that the people who fail do not do so because they want to fail; they fail because they *do not know how to succeed.* In answer to that lack of key information, this verse tells us how to succeed. It is God's guaranteed pathway to success.

THE WAY TO SUCCESS

We have seen that most of God's promises come with certain conditions that must be met in order for the promises to be fulfilled. Let us look at the conditions given in Joshua 1:8. First, "*This book of the law shall not depart from your mouth.*" Please notice the word "*mouth.*" We need to speak God's Word, not merely read it. Second, God declares, "*You shall meditate on it day and night.*" Meditation refers to the heart and mind—to our inner being. Third, "*So that you may be careful to do according to all that is written in it.*" Three significant words in this verse are "*mouth,*" "*meditate,*" and "*do.*" In other words (and I will change the exact order for a moment), you must *think* God's law, *speak* God's law, and *act on* God's law. Right meditation, right speaking, and right action— and the "rightness" is determined by being in accordance with God's principles.

Joshua only had the first five books of the Bible, called the Pentateuch, which are the books of Moses. However, we have a much more complete revelation of God and His ways. We have the total Bible, containing sixty-six books. If the five books of Moses would do that much for Joshua, how much should we anticipate from the total revelation of all sixty-six books of the Bible! Our revelation is greater—but the principles by which we must live are the same. We need to think, speak, and act according to God's Word.

CONFESS AND BELIEVE; BELIEVE AND CONFESS

In the New Testament, while stating the requirements for salvation, Paul said this about the Word of God:

> But what does it say? "The Word is near you, in your mouth and in your heart"—that is, the word of faith which we are preaching, that if you confess with your mouth Jesus as Lord, and believe in your heart that God raised Him from the dead, you shall be saved; for with the heart man believes, resulting in righteousness, and with the mouth he confesses, resulting in salvation.   (Romans 10:8–10 NASB)

A more literal translation of verse 10 would be "...with the heart man believes to righteousness and with the mouth he confesses to salvation." Notice that in this passage, there is a continual joining together of the heart and the mouth. The order in which Paul presents these truths is very important. But first, we must understand two vital words.

The word *confess* has a special meaning in the Bible. Its literal meaning is "to say the same as." When we confess, we are saying the same as God says in His Word, whether it is about sin, salvation, healing, prayer, or anything else. Confession is making the words of our mouth agree with the Word of God.

The word *salvation* is an all-inclusive term that covers all the benefits provided for us through the death of Jesus Christ on the cross. It includes spiritual, physical, and material benefits in this life and in the next—in time and in eternity. Bearing this in mind, we must look at what Paul says in this passage about the relationship between the mouth and the heart. He uses this pair of words three times, once in each verse. In verse 8, he writes, "*The word is* *near you, in your **mouth** and in your **heart**.*" Notice that "*mouth*" comes first, and then "*heart*." Next, in verse 9, he says, "*That if you confess with your **mouth** Jesus as Lord, and believe in your **heart** that God raised Him from the dead, you shall be saved.*" Again, the mouth comes before the heart. However, in verse 10, where Paul uses that pair of words for the third time, he reverses the order, so that the heart comes before the mouth: "*for with the **heart** man believes, resulting in righteousness, and with the **mouth** he confesses, resulting in salvation.*"

I believe there is a very practical reason for this sequence. Many times, the way to become convinced of God's truth in our experience is to make the right confession. There may be times when you do not feel in your heart that you fully believe a particular truth of God's Word. However, you still believe it is God's Word, and you trust that His Word is true. In such a case, because God says it, you are willing to say it. In so doing, you humble yourself, abasing your own carnal mind before the authority of the Word of God. Since God's Word says it, you say it with your mouth—and, from your mouth, it moves into your heart. If you continue to say it with your mouth, over time, it becomes established in your heart.

Once it is established in your heart, it is natural for you to continue to say it. Because it is now in your heart, it comes up out of your heart and into your mouth. This is how you establish yourself in the truth of God's Word. For example, you confess yourself into the salvation of God—first from the mouth to the heart, and then from the heart back to the mouth. "*Confession is made unto salvation*" (Romans 10:10 KJV). After God's truth is established in both your mouth and your heart, you act it out in your life. James tells us:

> *In the same way, faith by itself, if it is not accompanied by action, is dead.*   (James 2:17 NIV)

As the body without the spirit is dead, so faith without deeds is dead.   (James 2:26 NIV)

It is not enough merely to believe the Word and say it—you must also act it out. This brings us back to the same principles that were established for Joshua: *think* God's Word, *speak* God's Word, and *act on* God's Word. The result is guaranteed: *success.*

In part three of this book, we will examine promises that are designed by God to meet particular needs we face in our lives. One of the greatest and most fundamental needs we all have is to know our sins have been forgiven. We will begin the next section of this book focusing on that vital need.

INHERITING THE BLESSINGS

This book of the law shall not depart from your mouth, but you shall meditate on it day and night, so that you may be careful to do according to all that is written in it; for then you will make your way prosperous, and then you will have success.   (Joshua 1:8 NASB)

But what does it say? "The Word is near you, in your mouth and in your heart"—that is, the word of faith which we are preaching, that if you confess with your mouth Jesus as Lord, and believe in your heart that God raised Him from the dead, you shall be saved; for with the heart man believes, resulting in righteousness, and with the mouth he confesses, resulting in salvation.   (Romans 10:8–10 NASB)

PART THREE:

APPLYING GOD'S PROMISES

12

RECEIVING FORGIVENESS

As we set out on our journey through the land of God's promises, we will be identifying particular needs or problems that commonly arise in our lives. I hope to present, in very practical ways, how you and I can meet our needs and solve our problems by locating and claiming the specific promises of God that are applicable for each situation. In my many years of walking with the Lord, I have come to appreciate that He is a very practical God. I have discovered that anything which is truly spiritual is also extremely practical for everyday living. We sometimes talk of people who are "so heavenly minded, they are of no earthly use." But such people are not truly spiritual. People who are truly led by the Holy Spirit tend to be very practical.

THE PROBLEM OF SIN

The basic issue of our entire spiritual life, as addressed in the Word of God, is the *problem of sin*. Therefore, confronted with the reality of our sin, an enormous question emerges: How can we be sure God will forgive us? We can be sure of it because one of the greatest promises of our inheritance is the forgiveness of sin.

Our first step is to *face the fact of sin*. The Bible is very clear about this: *there is no one who has not sinned*. Sin applies to people of all races, all faiths, and all backgrounds. It is a malady we all have in common. Solomon says, *"There is no man who does not sin"* (1 Kings 8:46 NASB). And the prophet Isaiah says, *"All of us like sheep have gone astray, each of us has turned to his own way"* (Isaiah 53:6 NASB). Notice how emphatic and all-inclusive those words in Isaiah are: *"all of us"* and *"each of us."* We have all gone astray. The essence of going astray is not necessarily that we have committed some heinous sin like murder or adultery. Rather, we have indulged one tendency that all of us have in common: we have been stubborn, self-willed, and disobedient toward God. Every person has turned to his or her own way. And, clearly, our own way is not God's way.

FALLING SHORT

In the New Testament, Paul writes, *"For all have sinned and fall short of the glory of God"* (Romans 3:23 NASB, NIV). Once again, we see that the essence of sin is not necessarily some terrible crime. It is simply falling short of God's glory.

It is important that we truly understand the heart of sin. Sin is a failure to live according to the laws of God. It is a failure to fulfill the purpose for which God created us. He created us so we might have the unspeakable privilege of living for His glory and bringing glory to Him as our Maker. When we sin, we rob God of that glory.

I believe we can better understand sin by viewing it in this way—as a failure to fulfill the function for which we were created by God. Furthermore, I would define sin as "a failure for which we are accountable." We cannot excuse ourselves by saying we could not help sinning. We are responsible for our sin.

THE PROGNOSIS OF SIN

Let us now consider the prognosis of sin. *Prognosis,* of course, is a medical term referring to the likely outcome of a disease. The doctor first diagnoses your disease and then tells you the course— or the prognosis—your disease is likely to follow. The prognosis of sin in the Bible is very clear. There is no doubt about the course the disease of sin will take. In Romans 6:23, Paul writes, *"For the wages of sin is death"* (NASB, NIV).

"Wages" are what we earn for what we do. To put it bluntly, then, what we have all earned for the sins we have committed is death. That fact is clear, emphatic, simple, and undeniable. It is a spiritual law.

In James 1:13–15, we read these words:

> Let no one say when he is tempted, "I am being tempted by God"; for God cannot be tempted by evil, and He Himself does not tempt anyone. But each one is tempted when he is carried away and enticed by his own lust. Then when lust has conceived, it gives birth to sin; and when sin is accomplished, it brings forth death.   (NASB)

James very carefully closes the door to our putting the blame upon God for the fact that we have done wrong. He says, *"God cannot be tempted by evil, and He Himself does not tempt anyone* [with evil]." When we are tempted, it is our own lust and perverted desires that carry us away and entice us into sin. Then, in agreement with Paul, James gives us the prognosis of sin by saying, *"It brings forth death."*

A progressive order is revealed in this passage. When we yield to lust (perverted desire), it produces sin. When we continue in that sin, it produces death. This death does not merely refer to the cessation of physical life. It is also a spiritual condition of alienation and separation from God, which may become eternal. If we reach the point where we continue in sin, tragically, there may be no turning back.

THE BURDEN OF SIN

There is something else we must deal with when we have gone astray: the *burden* of sin. This reality is vividly stated by David in the Psalms. David was a righteous man at heart, but he also knew what it was to sin grievously and then to repent and return to find God's mercy. Here is what he expresses about the burden of sin in Psalm 32:

> *When I kept silent about my sin, my body wasted away through my groaning all day long. For day and night Thy hand was heavy upon me; my vitality was drained away as with the fever heat of summer. I acknowledged my sin to Thee, and my iniquity I did not hide; I said, "I will confess my transgressions to the Lord"; and Thou didst forgive the guilt of my sin.* (Psalm 32:3–5 NASB)

Thank God for that last statement! "*Thou didst forgive the guilt of my sin.*" However, notice what David went through before he confessed his sin: "*My body wasted away through my groaning all day long.… My vitality was drained away.*" Sin produced an impact on his whole being. David repeats this theme in another psalm, where he says to the Lord:

> *Because of Your wrath there is no health in my body; my bones have no soundness because of my sin. My guilt has overwhelmed me like a burden too heavy to bear.*
> (Psalm 38:3–4 NIV)

Have you ever felt like David did? Have you felt that your sin and guilt have become a burden too heavy to bear? Perhaps you are feeling that right now. If so, there is good news for you. There is a way you can be delivered from that burden of guilt and be free from it forever.

GOD'S PROMISE OF FORGIVENESS

We have considered the fact of sin, the prognosis of sin, and the burden of sin. Now we turn to God's promises of forgiveness. We will look at two specific promises, one from the Old Testament and one from the New Testament.

He who conceals his sins does not prosper, but whoever confesses and renounces them finds mercy.

(Proverbs 28:13 NIV)

The result expressed in the first part of this verse is exactly the opposite of the promise God gave to Joshua when he was about to lead the Israelites into the promised land. That promise was, in effect, "If you will do what I tell you, you will make your way prosperous, and you will have success." (See Joshua 1:8.) Thus, what is one inevitable barrier to true prosperity? Sin—if we hold on to it and do not confess and renounce it. *"He who conceals his sins does not prosper."* Please bear that in mind, because it is very important. However, also remember the wonderful promise of the second half of Proverbs 28:13: *"whoever confesses and renounces* [his sins] *finds mercy."*

God promises us mercy if we meet two conditions: first, *confess*, and second, *renounce*. He requires that we honestly acknowledge to Him the sins we have committed. I have met some people who had the impression that if they did not tell God about their sins, He might never know about them! Of course, that is ridiculous. God does not ask us to confess for His sake but for our sake.

When we honestly and humbly confess our sin before God, acknowledging it as wrong, we are agreeing with what His Word says about sin. Bringing it out into the open, we invite God to deal with it and deliver us from it. However, if we hold on to it and try to keep it concealed, we shut off the way for God to help us deal with it.

To be free of our sin, we must also renounce it and let it go. How do we do that? By turning from it. We must decide we do not want to go on committing sins of that kind any longer. This is a decision of the will, and so our will is involved in this transaction with God. If we do not make a definite decision, according to the conditions God has set for us, we cannot experience God's mercy.

Now that we have examined the Old Testament passage regarding forgiveness, let's look at the New Testament promise:

> *If we confess our sins, He [God] is faithful and just and will forgive us our sins and purify us from all unrighteousness.*
> (1 John 1:9 NIV)

In this passage, as well, we see that God requires us to confess our sins. When we meet that condition, Scripture promises we will see two attributes of God—that He is faithful, and that He is just. We must understand how those attributes work together.

God is *faithful* to forgive us, because He has promised to do so, and God will never go back on His promise if we meet His conditions. He is also *just* to forgive us because He has already visited the penalty for all our sins upon Jesus. When Jesus hung on the cross and died, He paid the full and final punishment for the sins of the whole human race. Therefore, if we meet God's conditions—if we confess, repent, and turn to Him—He is able to forgive us totally and finally without compromising His own divine justice.

In summary, to enjoy the benefits of God's forgiveness, we must meet three requirements: (1) we must confess our sins; (2) we must renounce our sins; and (3) by faith, we must receive God's forgiveness, believing that, according to His faithfulness and justice, He will do exactly what He has promised!

WHAT IS YOUR BURDEN?

As you have been reading this chapter, perhaps you have become aware that you are carrying a sense of guilt, shame, or failure about your sins. They may be sins from the past or sins with which you are presently struggling—but, in some way, you are feeling the burden. Perhaps you think God is looking at you with displeasure because of your sins and failures.

If this outlook applies to you in any measure, I want to give you the opportunity to open your heart to God and receive complete forgiveness. Do you want to be thoroughly cleansed of your guilt through the work of the blood of Jesus Christ? It is very simple to receive this cleansing. But it takes faith. You cannot go by how you feel. You must look to the cross of Jesus Christ and the completeness of the work of redemption He accomplished on your behalf.

If you would like to bring all of your guilty feelings to God, the following prayer is written just for you. Meditate on it for a moment and let it sink into your heart. Within the prayer, there is an opportunity for you to mention specific sins, if that is appropriate. Do not, however, become introspective or morbid about your sins. Deal only with those sins where there is a problem with guilt or which the Holy Spirit brings to your mind. Then, simply pray a prayer of faith—either as I have written it below or one in your own words. Before you pray, remember the promise of 1 John 1:9: *"If we confess our sins, He* [God] *is faithful and just and will forgive us our sins and purify us from all unrighteousness"* (NIV). His promises are true!

After you have prayed, regardless of how you feel, *believe* that God has completed His work, and continue to thank Him for the forgiveness He has given you.

> Heavenly Father, I come to You in the name of Jesus. I thank You for sending Jesus to die on the cross and shed His precious blood for me. I believe that Jesus took all my

sin upon Himself, and that all the guilt that was due me for my sin was charged to Him. Therefore, based on the promise of Your Word, I first confess that I have sinned. [You may want to mention any specific sins for which you feel guilty or which the Holy Spirit brings to your mind.] Regarding these sins, I thank You for Your forgiveness—based on Your promise that if I would confess them, You would forgive them. Taking You at Your Word, I proclaim that not only am I forgiven, but, through the blood of Jesus, I have also been cleansed from all unrighteousness. I declare all this to be true for me, in the name of Jesus! Thank You, Lord! Amen.

INHERITING THE BLESSINGS

He who conceals his sins does not prosper, but whoever confesses and renounces them finds mercy.

(Proverbs 28:13 NIV)

If we confess our sins, He [God] is faithful and just and will forgive us our sins and purify us from all unrighteousness.

(1 John 1:9 NIV)

13

BECOMING A CHILD OF GOD

Acknowledging the problem of sin in our lives, and receiving God's forgiveness through Jesus Christ, is foundational for establishing a personal relationship with our heavenly Father. Yet there is another need that is vital for our spiritual health and growth: we must understand what it means to be a child of God.

THE PROCESS OF NEW BIRTH

To gain that understanding, we will begin by looking at a conversation between Jesus and a religious leader of His day, a Pharisee named Nicodemus. This remarkable conversation is recorded in the gospel of John:

Now there was a man of the Pharisees, named Nicodemus, a ruler of the Jews; this man came to Him by night, and said to Him, "Rabbi, we know that You have come from God as a teacher; for no one can do these signs that You do unless God is with him." Jesus answered and said to him, "Truly, truly, I say to you, unless one is born again, he cannot see the kingdom of God." Nicodemus said to Him, "How can a man be born when he is old? He cannot enter a second time into his

mother's womb and be born, can he?" Jesus answered, "Truly,
truly, I say to you, unless one is born of water and the Spirit,
he cannot enter into the kingdom of God. That which is born
of the flesh is flesh, and that which is born of Spirit is spirit.
Do not marvel that I said to you, 'You must be born again.'
The wind blows where it wishes and you hear the sound of it,
but do not know where it comes from and where it is going; so
is everyone who is born of the Spirit." Nicodemus answered
and said to Him, "How can these things be?" Jesus answered
and said to him, "Are you the teacher of Israel, and do not
understand these things? Truly, truly, I say to you, we speak
that which we know, and bear witness of that which we have
seen; and you do not receive our witness."

(John 3:1–11 NASB)

I have always found it interesting that even though Nicodemus
was obviously a sincere, good, intelligent, and educated man, he
simply could not understand what Jesus was talking about. Yet
Jesus was obviously speaking about one of the most important
moments in life—an experience He described as "[being] *born
again.*" Other Bible versions use the phrase "*born from above,*" or
"*born anew.*" These are all legitimate translations.

This experience is so important that, as Jesus declared to
Nicodemus, unless a person goes through this process—is born
again—he or she cannot see and enter the kingdom of God. Of
course, this statement shocked Nicodemus greatly! He tried ear-
nestly to find out what Jesus meant by it.

Jesus explained that there are essentially two different types
of human nature: there is a fleshly, physical nature, and there is
a spiritual nature: "*That which is born of the flesh is flesh, and that
which is born of Spirit is spirit.*"

Hearing about the new-birth process Jesus described,
Nicodemus somehow thought he would have to go back again

into his mother's womb and be born as an infant. But Jesus said, in effect, "I am not speaking about a birth that produces a fleshly nature. That you already have. I am speaking about a birth that produces a spiritual nature you have not yet experienced."

LIKE THE WIND

To further explain spiritual birth, Jesus used an illustration from nature—the wind, one of the most familiar elements in our physical world. He said, *"The wind blows where it wishes and you hear the sound of it, but you do not know where it comes from and where it is going; so is everyone who is born of the Spirit"* (John 3:8 NASB).

Both the Hebrew of the Old Testament and the Greek of the New Testament have one word that can mean either *wind, breath,* or *spirit.* Therefore, when Jesus used the wind as an example, He was directing us to what the example illustrates, which is the behavior of the Holy Spirit. He was saying, "The Holy Spirit is like the wind. Nobody tells the wind where to blow. It comes into our lives, but we don't know where it comes from, and we don't know where it is going." Then He added, "In the new birth, that is what the work of the Holy Spirit is like." We do not know where the Spirit comes from, and we do not know where He goes, but we do know something about what He does.

EVIDENCE OF THE SPIRIT

I was once talking to a man who was very argumentative, and he told me, "I don't believe in anything I can't see!"

"Well," I answered, "that's ridiculous! You've never seen the wind, but you believe in the wind, don't you?" He was stumped for an answer!

None of us has ever seen the wind. So how do we know where the wind is blowing? We can see *what it does* and thus know the direction in which it is moving. We see it cause the clouds to scud across the sky, the dust to rise up in the street, and the trees to bend and sway. We might see the wind blow a hat off someone's head so that he or she has to go running after it. All of these indicators—and many other evidences—prove that the wind is operating in the world around us.

Jesus was telling Nicodemus that this is what people experience when they are born again. The Spirit of God comes into their lives, and they don't really understand where He comes from or where He is going. But they are aware that certain changes have happened within them.

When I was a pastor in London in the 1950s, a young Danish woman, who was just a nominal churchgoer, came to our home to find out more about what it meant to be born again. My first wife, Lydia, and I instructed her and explained what she had to do to have this experience. Then I led her in a very simple prayer in which she did what God required of her. She was a rather formal type of person, not in any sense emotional, which, in my experience, is typical of most Danish people. But after she had bowed her head and said the prayer, as she lifted her head, two large teardrops appeared in her eyes and trickled down her cheeks. Rather self-consciously, she dabbed her eyes with her handkerchief. Then two more tears appeared and trickled down her cheeks, and she said, "I don't know why I'm crying."

"You see," I explained, "the wind has just started to blow."

This was one of the evidences that the Holy Spirit was at work in her life. She experienced a sense of tenderness, a sense of relief, and a sense of joy she could neither explain nor understand. She was almost embarrassed. But it was so real that she could not hide it.

I am sure Jesus gave the same explanation about the new birth to many people besides the Pharisee Nicodemus. But I believe the conversation with Nicodemus is recorded for a special reason. If there had been any other requirements besides the new birth that would have brought spiritual life, Nicodemus would have done them all. He was a religious man, he was educated, he held a high social position, and he belonged to the Jewish race, a people God had set apart for special purposes. It is important to note, however, that neither religion, education, social position, nor racial prominence is any substitute for the new birth.

THE KEY TRANSACTION

So far, I have explained two principles: the necessity of being born again and the nature of what happens when it takes place. However, there still remains one very important question: How can a person be born again? In the first chapter of John's gospel, the apostle says this about Jesus:

> *He came to His own, and those who were His own did not receive Him.*　　　　　　　　　　　(John 1:11 NASB)

Jesus came as a Jew to the Jewish people (although, ultimately, He came for all people). Yet, as a nation—not as individuals— as a collective nation, they rejected Him who was their Messiah. However, we can thank God there is a *"But…"* after the verse cited above.

> *But as many as received Him [Jesus], to them He gave the right to become children of God, even to those who believe in His name, who were born not of blood, nor of the will of the flesh, nor of the will of man, but of God.*
>
> 　　　　　　　　　　　　　　　(John 1:12–13 NASB)

In the above passage, notice that John excludes three possibilities for being born of God. First, He says that the new birth is *"not of blood."* It is not by natural descent. No matter how good your father and mother are, or were, that does not make you good in the spiritual sense. You must have a spiritual birth in which you receive a new nature.

Second, John says the new birth is not *"of the will of the flesh."* It is not the result of the normal means of human procreation.

Third, he says it is not *"of the will of man."* The original word that is translated as *"man"* is the term the Greeks used for a husband. In other words, it is not the result of a man deciding he wishes to have a family. It is on a different plane; it is not physical but spiritual.

What, then, is the transaction that leads to being born again, or being born of God? Everyone who desires to be born of God must do what is summed up in this very simple statement: *"As many as received Him...."* The one decision you must make in order to be born again is to receive Jesus as your personal Savior and confess Him as your Lord. When you do that, He gives you the right and the authority to become a child of God.

You receive Him through faith—through simply believing in His name. Jesus cannot be received by doing religious good works or by any claim you may have of your own righteousness. He is received only through believing in His name—with the result that you are born of God!

INVITE JESUS IN

As we close this chapter, I want to give you a promise that you can lay hold of if you desire to be born again. It is given by Jesus in Revelation 3:20:

> *Behold, I stand at the door and knock; if anyone hears My voice and opens the door, I will come in to him, and will dine with him, and he with Me.* (NASB)

This is a promise for you. Jesus is standing outside your heart's door and knocking. He is a gentleman. He will not force His way in. If you want Him to come into your heart, you must invite Him in. And if you invite Him in, you can be sure He will come in—because He keeps His word. He says, *"I will come in to him, and will dine with him, and he with Me."*

Thus, you receive Jesus by inviting Him in. You open the door to Him, and yield to Him as He enters. Then, in faith, you thank Him that He has come in. This is saving faith: simply believing that Jesus will do what He said He would do, if you would believe in Him.

Perhaps you have never made a conscious decision to open the door of your heart, invite Jesus in, and allow Him to become the Lord of your life. You may attend church, and perhaps you even pray and read the Bible faithfully. Yet, as beneficial as these activities can be, they do not make you a child of God.

If you have any question at all about whether Jesus lives inside you in a very personal and real way, I encourage you to settle the issue once and for all by receiving Him into your heart by faith right now.

Below, I present a simple prayer for inviting Jesus into your heart. Read it and meditate on it. If it expresses the desire of your heart, pray it as it is written. Or you may simply express a prayer in your own words.

Lord Jesus, I thank You that You died for my sins on the cross so I might be forgiven. I acknowledge that You were buried and rose from the dead so I might have life with You forever. I now open the door of my heart and ask You to come in and live inside me forever. I turn my life over to You, and I ask You to begin leading me by Your Holy Spirit so I can know You better and walk with You. Thank You for coming into my heart according to the promise of Your Word. Amen.

If you prayed that prayer, you can be sure Jesus has answered it—He has come into your heart. Why not begin thanking Him now? Tell Him you seek to involve Him personally in every area of your life.

The rest of this book will help you begin to claim the promises of your inheritance as a child of God and to experience His grace more fully in every area of your life.

INHERITING THE BLESSINGS

But as many as received Him [Jesus], to them He gave the right to become children of God, even to those who believe in His name, who were born not of blood, nor of the will of the flesh, nor of the will of man, but of God.
(John 1:12–13 NASB)

Behold, I stand at the door and knock; if anyone hears My voice and opens the door, I will come in to him, and will dine with him, and he with Me.   (Revelation 3:20 NASB)

14

RELEASE FROM
MENTAL TORMENT

We continue our walk through the land of God's promises—identifying specific scriptural remedies for everyday issues we face. One of the most prevalent issues of the contemporary world is the problem of recurring mental torment. In this chapter, I want to share how to obtain release from negative mental bombardment, which many people seem to be confronted with on a daily basis.

COMMON LIFE PRESSURES

In our modern age, we are exposed to many different pressures—and these demands always seem to be increasing, never diminishing. The entire list of pressures we face would be far too numerous to attempt to name. However, I want to mention some simple but common examples.

1. Peer pressure from our particular group of friends or colleagues, from those in our age group, or from those on our social level. This is the pressure to conform and be like the rest of the group. Such pressure is manifested in a very obvious way among

schoolchildren. There can be enormous pressure to "do what all the other kids are doing."

For instance, young people may be pressured into using drugs or becoming sexually active because many of their friends are experimenting in those ways. If a young person refuses to do what everybody else is doing, they are made to feel very self-conscious.

Peer pressure continues as we grow older. It is commonly known as "keeping up with the Joneses." The other family across the street has a new car, so we need a new car. The next-door neighbor just put in a swimming pool, so we need a swimming pool.

Thus, in our culture, there is an almost ceaseless pressure to be like others, which is reinforced strongly by images in advertising and entertainment. These pressures are often contrary to our own inner nature and real personality.

2. The pressure to earn enough money to satisfy our material desires and to provide some security for our old age. There are continual demands to get and accumulate money—and, usually, no matter how much wealth people gain, it never seems to be enough.

3. The pressure just to survive. For example, many people face a constant fight against disease and illness. Some have been diagnosed with conditions that, in the shorter or longer term, may well prove fatal. It may be that you are currently fighting a disease, and the doctor's prognosis is that it is incurable; perhaps you have been told you may have only a few months or a few years to live. This amounts to a kind of death sentence that seems to hang over you. That can be one of the heaviest forms of pressure a person can face.

THREATENING, ACCUSING, TORTUROUS THOUGHTS

When facing such pressures, it is very common to experience the additional stress of dealing with an inner, tormenting voice.

Sometimes, it may seem like an audible voice, but most of the time, it is an inner one. What the voice says might be formulated in clear and specific sentences—sending a steady stream of threatening, accusing, or torturous thoughts.

It is important to understand that where there is a voice, there is a person behind the voice. There is no such phenomenon in the universe as a voice without a person. The presence of a voice indicates the presence of a personality. When the voice we hear in our thoughts accuses or torments us in some way, then we know one fact for sure: *the person behind that voice is Satan, the devil.* Bear in mind that the devil is the accuser and the tormentor. (See, for example, Revelation 12:10.) When you have an accusing, tormenting voice in your mind that pressures you, drives you, and goads you, it should be clear to you without further evidence that its source is the devil.

COMMON ATTACKS AGAINST THE MIND

The following are common forms of accusation and torment the devil brings against people's minds. I have encountered each one of these examples more than once as I have counseled people who were under mental pressure or experiencing mental torment.

1. "God doesn't love you." The ultimate result of believing this accusation is to feel rejected and lonely. You might begin to think that other people are able to easily relate to God—but you can't. You might feel like God seems to have a plan for other people's lives—but not for you.

2. "You are a failure" or "You'll always be a failure." It may be that these accusing words come not only from a voice in your mind but also from another person—maybe your parents or even your spouse. Either way, the message is clear and constant: "You have failed so many times that there just doesn't seem to be any alternative for you in life but failure."

3. "You are losing your mind." In counseling sessions, I have been astonished at how many people have heard a voice speaking these words to them. It usually goes something like this: "You know, your aunt died in a mental hospital, and there was something strange about your grandmother—you're going to be the next one." I do not think it is possible to put into words how agonizing that kind of torment is.

4. "You have a fatal illness." There can be tormenting thoughts associated with physical pain or symptoms of a possible disease. The voice inside may tell you, "That pain you feel is caused by cancer." Maybe you have other symptoms that make you too frightened to go to the doctor for an examination. Ceaselessly, day and night, as you experience those symptoms, you battle the thought that has formed in your mind: "This pain is caused by some form of terminal illness." Quite possibly, there is very little wrong with you. However, you are just too shaken and frightened by the pain to face up to the challenge of the torment. It keeps you from rising up to refute those nagging thoughts.

Job is an Old Testament character who underwent the type of torment we are dealing with in this chapter. He summed up the process very vividly and succinctly when he lamented:

> What I feared has come upon me; what I dreaded has happened to me. I have no peace, no quietness; I have no rest, but only turmoil.　　　　　　　　　　　　　　(Job 3:25–26 NIV)

What Job said is true of countless thousands in our contemporary society: "*What I feared has come upon me.*" Fear can open the door to the very condition you are dreading. One of the possible causes of cancer in some people is simply their morbid fear of it. Likewise, one factor that may contribute to insanity in some people is their fear of losing their mind. The devil uses fear as a lever to bring additional difficulties upon us.

DOORS OF ATTACK

"What I feared has come upon me; what I dreaded has happened to me. I have no peace, no quietness; I have no rest, but only turmoil." Is that your condition? If Job's words describe your state of mind in any way, I want you to know there is a remedy. It comes as we recognize the door Satan is using to get into our lives. He uses various doors, but I am going to suggest two of the most common, which I have seen over and over in counseling sessions. The first door is *resentment* and *unforgiveness*. It is common to feel resentful and unforgiving toward someone. Often, it is a person who is close to us or who was close to us at one time in our lives, such as a parent, spouse, child, neighbor, or minister in the church.

The second door Satan frequently uses is an attitude of *rebellion*—especially against God. The rebellion might be against society or any form of human authority. But in its essence, it is rebellion against God—a refusal to submit to His righteous government as it is expressed in the family, the church, or society.

CLOSING THE DOORS

If Satan is taking advantage of an open door to get into our lives, the most logical solution is simply to close that door. Suppose a wild animal were going in and out of the front door to your home. The problem wouldn't be solved merely by yelling at the animal or praying for deliverance—you would need to close the door so it could no longer come in. Many people try to rebuke the devil or pray for deliverance yet fail to block his entry into their lives.

If the door Satan is using is resentment and unforgiveness, then we must forgive the person we resent. We must lay down any bitterness or hatred, remembering these words of Jesus in the Lord's Prayer: *"Forgive us our debts, as we also have forgiven our debtors"* (Matthew 6:12 NASB, NIV). We have no right to ask God to forgive us beyond the measure in which we forgive others. Jesus comments on this truth in the sixth chapter of Matthew:

> *For if you forgive men when they sin against you, your heavenly Father will also forgive you. But if you do not forgive men their sins, your Father will not forgive your sins.*
> (Matthew 6:14–15 NIV)

Therefore, if we want forgiveness from God, we must forgive others. God has laid down that requirement, and He will not alter it. Please realize that forgiveness is not an emotion—*it is a decision.* In a sense, it is tearing up the IOU for what somebody owes you. You have that individual's IOU in your hand, but God has a great many IOUs from you in His hand. He says simply, "You tear up your IOU, and I'll tear up Mine."

If the door Satan is using is rebellion, and especially rebellion against God, the way to close that door is to submit to God. Again, this is a decision of your will. James says, *"Submit yourselves, then, to God. Resist the devil, and he will flee from you"* (James 4:7 NIV). You cannot resist the devil as long as you are resisting God— because God is the only One who can give you the faith, strength, and grace you need to resist the devil. Thus, if the devil has been tormenting you, your first step is to submit to God. Lay down your rebellion against Him and say, "Lord, I yield to You. You are my Creator; You are in command of the universe, and I submit to Your dealings in my life. I will do whatever You require of me."

At this point—when you have submitted to God and made that your confession—you have the right to take the sword of the Spirit, which is the Word of God (see Ephesians 6:17), and drive the devil out of your life. You can stand against the adversary the same way Jesus did in the wilderness temptation. Each time the enemy came to tempt Him, Jesus gave this reply: *"It is written...."* (See, for example, Matthew 4:4, 7, 10.) Because Jesus was submitted to God, He could resist the devil.

If you submit to God the way Jesus did, then you, also, have the right to resist the devil. You have the right to say to those voices, "I will not listen to you anymore. Satan, get out of my life! I am yielded to God. I belong to God. You have no power over me! All the claims against me were settled by the death of Jesus on the cross. I now resist you and command you to leave me."

In this chapter, we have learned practical ways to identify mental torment and find freedom from it. But this question still remains: How can we come to enjoy true peace of mind? That is our next theme as we continue our journey through the land of God's promises.

INHERITING THE BLESSINGS

For if you forgive men when they sin against you, your heavenly Father will also forgive you. But if you do not forgive men their sins, your Father will not forgive your sins.
(Matthew 6:14–15 NIV)

Submit yourselves, then, to God. Resist the devil, and he will flee from you. (James 4:7 NIV)

15

TRUE PEACE OF MIND

In the process of opening our hearts and minds to the promises in God's Word, we find the answers we need to the common problems and issues of life. We have just seen how the promises of God can release us from mental torment. A subject that very naturally follows is how to enjoy true peace of mind. These two topics fit together like opposite sides of a single coin—one negative and the other positive. How to obtain release from mental torment is the negative side. How to enjoy true peace of mind is the positive side. Clearly, we need the positive just as much as the negative.

It is not enough merely to rid our minds of mental torment. Although we will experience relief, in time, we might also experience a kind of mental vacuum. Almost invariably, if we continue in that vacuum long enough, some evil force will press its way in and afflict our minds. Therefore, an essential part of our protection is to have our minds garrisoned with the *peace of God*.

WE HAVE PEACE WITH GOD

The first and most important peace of mind we need is the assurance that we are at peace with God. We can have no real or permanent peace unless it issues out of a right relationship with almighty God. In two separate places in the book of Isaiah, the Lord says, "*There is no peace for the wicked.*" (See Isaiah 48:22 NASB, NIV, NKJV; 57:21 NASB, NIV, NKJV.) For those who are in rebellion or opposition against God, leading lives that are not subjected to His laws and requirements, there is no peace. In fact, there is no way that such persons can have peace. In order to have true peace of mind, we must first make sure that we have been reconciled with our heavenly Father.

In Romans 5:1, Paul says, "*Therefore having been justified by faith, we have peace with God through our Lord Jesus Christ*" (NASB). Further on in that chapter, Paul says that through Jesus, "*we have now received the reconciliation*" (verse 11 NASB). We had a definite need for reconciliation. By our carnal nature and sinful lives, we were at war with almighty God. We were not in submission to His just ordinances and requirements. We were not leading the kind of life that brought glory to Him. Therefore, we had to repent and accept the reconciliation that is extended to us by God through Jesus Christ.

On the cross, Jesus was identified with our sin and rebellion. The judgment for that sin came upon Him, and He paid the full and final penalty for our sins. How, then, have we been reconciled to God? Through the death of Jesus on our behalf.

WE HAVE BEEN JUSTIFIED

Having been reconciled to God, and having received His promise of forgiveness, we have been "*justified by faith*" (Romans 5:1 NASB, NKJV, KJV), so that we now have peace with God. "*Justified*" is an important word. It could be interpreted, "We have been acquitted. We are no longer held guilty" or "We have been rendered righteous." When we believe in Jesus and His death on our behalf, His righteousness is imputed (or reckoned) to us, on the basis of our faith.

Personally, this is the definition of "justified" that I like best: *just-as-if-I'd never sinned.* That is beautiful, isn't it? When the righteousness of Jesus has been reckoned to me by God, then I am righteous—not with my own righteousness but with Jesus's righteousness. Please bear in mind that the righteousness of Jesus never knew sin or guilt. The only reason He paid the penalty was to pay it on our behalf. He had no penalty to pay for Himself.

Therefore, begin to think in terms of being justified. Say to yourself, "I have been justified, just-as-if-I'd never sinned. I have peace with God. God holds nothing more against me. I have been acquitted." If you find this hard to believe, say these declarations again and again until you know in your heart that you believe them.

GOD IS FOR US

Knowing we have peace with God is the true basis for mental peace. Once we have this assurance and know that God is on our side, it makes all the difference in life. In Romans 8:31–32, speaking on behalf of those of us who have received this reconciliation, Paul writes,

> *What then shall we say to these things? If God is for us, who is against us?* (Romans 8:31 NASB)

That is a good question! Who can be against us if God is for us? Someone has expressed it this way: "One plus God is a majority in any situation."

> *He who did not spare His own Son, but delivered Him up for us all, how will He not also with Him freely give us all things?* (Romans 8:32 NASB)

Because God was willing to give Jesus—His most precious treasure, His only begotten Son—we know that such love as that will never withhold from us anything that is good or that we need.

God is on our side. He is for us, and the resources of heaven are at our disposal. Once we really comprehend by faith that we have been reconciled with God, that we have been reckoned righteous with the righteousness of Jesus—justified, "just-as-if-I'd never sinned"—then we can move on into the complete and full provision of God for our mental peace.

THE PEACE OF GOD

This provision is stated as clearly by Paul in Philippians as anywhere else I know of:

> Be anxious for nothing, but in everything by prayer and supplication with thanksgiving let your requests be made known to God. And the peace of God, which surpasses all comprehension, shall guard your hearts and your minds in Christ Jesus.
> (Philippians 4:6–7 NASB)

Notice this significant and beautiful thought: "*The peace of God, which surpasses all comprehension, shall guard your hearts and your minds in Christ Jesus.*" This statement, which speaks of guarding your heart and mind, affirms what I said about the danger of a vacuum. You cannot leave your mind empty. If you do, some evil influence or pressure will come in.

You must fill your mind with the peace of God, and then the peace of God will guard your mind. The Greek word translated "*guard*" in the above verse means "to garrison" your mind. To garrison means to have troops stationed in a fortress or town in order to defend it. In other words, a supernatural peace from God stands watch over our minds so that no evil pressures or tormenting influences can find access. Paul gives further vital instructions in the next verse:

> Finally, brethren, whatever is true, whatever is honorable, whatever is right, whatever is pure, whatever is lovely,

*whatever is of good repute, if there is any excellence and if any-
thing worthy of praise, let your mind dwell on these things.*

(Philippians 4:8 NASB)

MEETING THE CONDITIONS

The prospect of receiving the very peace of God, which surpasses all comprehension as it guards our hearts and minds, is a
beautiful promise. We must remember, however, that in order to
claim this promise, we need to fulfill its conditions.

1. *Renounce anxiety.* The Scripture gives this order: *"Be anxious for nothing"* (Philippians 4:6 NASB). Every time anxiety begins
to move in on your mind, refuse it! Answer it by saying, "I am
justified, just-as-if-I'd never sinned. God holds nothing against me.
I have peace with God. God is on my side. All His resources are
available to me. I refuse to be anxious!" It is not sensible or logical
to be anxious when you believe that. Therefore, the first condition
is to *renounce anxiety.*

2. *Pray about everything.* "In everything by prayer and supplication..." (verse 6 NASB). You may be familiar with the old hymn
"What a Friend We Have in Jesus," which says:

O what peace we often forfeit,
O what needless pain we bear,
All because we do not carry
Everything to God in prayer![1]

Many times, we do not experience mental peace simply because
we do not pray. We get into a problem or situation, and we try to
handle it with our own strength. We neglect to pray and turn to
God for His wisdom and resources, which are available to us as
soon as we pray.

---

1. Joseph Medlicott Scriven, 1855.

3. *Always be thankful.* Being thankful is also absolutely essential. It is not enough to pray—we must pray to God *"with thanksgiving"* (Philippians 4:6 NASB). A thankful heart is usually a peaceful heart, but an ungrateful person really cannot know true and lasting peace. Ingratitude is contrary to the very nature of God.

4. *Think about the right things.* We must fill our minds with *uplifting* and *beneficial* thoughts. In Philippians 4:8 (NASB), Paul tells us the kinds of thoughts that qualify. First, *"whatever is true."* Bear in mind that something may be true, but it doesn't necessarily mean we should dwell on it. For example, we should not focus our thoughts on people's faults and failings, even though such thoughts may be true. It would be a good discipline to shift our focus to the good qualities they may possess.

Paul then continues the list of what we should think about: whatever is honorable, right, pure, lovely, and of good repute, all that is excellent or worthy of praise. He concludes, *"Let your mind dwell on these things."* You have the power to focus your mind on whatever you choose. You can dwell on negative ideas, topics, and memories, or you can dwell on what builds you up. If you continue to struggle with negative thoughts, call upon the Holy Spirit. Remember, you can ask Him to help you find what is positive and edifying, and focus on it.

Let me share a vivid illustration from nature. In many countries, there are two kinds of birds: those that feed on carrion (rotten meat), and those that feed on fresh meat. Each bird finds what it is looking for—and the same is true of our minds. We can feed our minds on "carrion," or we can feed them on "fresh meat." If you look for what is negative, dark, and discouraging, you will probably find it. But if you look for what is positive, good, uplifting, and edifying, you will find it. And the peace of God will guard your mind—you will have true mental peace.

PRAYING FOR PEACE OF MIND

If you desire to take practical steps to overcome mental torment and enjoy peace of mind, I invite you to pray the following prayer:

> Lord, I realize that I can move from the mental torment I have been battling into true peace of mind. I now take the steps to rebuke and resist the accusing voice of the enemy. I declare that You are for me, O God. I am justified by my faith in Jesus Christ, giving me peace with You. I renounce anxiety. From now on, I will pray first when issues arise. I will give thanks for all You have done for me, and I will focus my thoughts on what is good, true, and pure.
>
> Thank You, Lord, for providing me, in Your Word, with steps to escape mental torment and have true peace of mind. I choose that peace today, and I receive it by faith. Amen!

INHERITING THE BLESSINGS

He who did not spare His own Son, but delivered Him up for us all, how will He not also with Him freely give us all things? (Romans 8:32 NASB)

Be anxious for nothing, but in everything by prayer and supplication with thanksgiving let your requests be made known to God. And the peace of God, which surpasses all comprehension, shall guard your hearts and your minds in Christ Jesus. Finally, brethren, whatever is true, whatever is honorable, whatever is right, whatever is pure, whatever is lovely, whatever is of good repute, if there is any excellence and if anything worthy of praise, let your mind dwell on these things.
(Philippians 4:6–8 NASB)

16

WISDOM FOR
EVERYDAY LIFE

At this point in our journey through the land of God's promises, we are like the children of Israel moving through the promised land—as they are depicted halfway through the book of Joshua. After having gained many victories and much territory, God said to them, in effect, "Very much of the land remains to be possessed." (See Joshua 13:1–6.) The same is true for us as Christians. We have covered a lot of ground—but we have entered into only a small part of the provision God has made for us.

Let us continue our exploration of this rich and wonderful land by considering the particular kinds of promises that relate to practical wisdom. I have found that all of the wisdom unfolded in the Bible is applicable and useful for everyday living.

ALL THE TREASURES OF WISDOM

First, we must realize that wisdom is a major part of our total inheritance in Jesus Christ. For example, in Colossians 2:2–3, Paul makes the following statement regarding his prayers for the Christians in Laodicea and in other places:

My purpose is that they may be encouraged in heart and united in love, so that they may have the full riches of complete understanding, in order that they may know the mystery of God, namely, Christ, in whom are hidden all the treasures of wisdom and knowledge.   (Colossians 2:2–3 NIV)

Where is wisdom? These verses tell us. All the treasures of wisdom and knowledge are hidden in Jesus Christ. Before I came to know Jesus, I was a professor of philosophy at Cambridge University, and I was continually searching for wisdom. In reality, however, I was living on the scraps from the garbage heaps of human wisdom. When I came to know Jesus, I was delighted to discover that all the treasures of wisdom and knowledge are in Him. So I turned aside from those garbage heaps and scrap piles. I made up my mind that I would seek the wisdom that is in Jesus—the treasures of wisdom and knowledge that are in Him.

Moreover, in 1 Corinthians 1:30, Paul writes,

But by His [God's] doing you are in Christ Jesus [our whole inheritance is in Christ Jesus], who became to us wisdom from God, and righteousness and sanctification, and redemption.   (NASB)

The person of Jesus is our wisdom, and all our wisdom is in Him. Because He is the totality of our inheritance, He is also our righteousness, our sanctification (or holiness), and our redemption.

ASKING GOD FOR WISDOM

Another important promise concerning our inheritance of wisdom through Jesus Christ is found in James 1:5–8:

If any of you lacks wisdom, he should ask God, who gives generously to all without finding fault, and it will be given to him. But when he asks, he must believe and not doubt, because he who doubts is like a wave of the sea, blown and tossed by the wind. That man should not think he will receive anything from the Lord; he is a double-minded man, unstable in all he does. (NIV)

Within this passage is a very clear promise of wisdom in any situation in which we might need it. Whenever we lack wisdom, we should ask God, *"who gives generously to all without finding fault."* God does not find fault with us for lacking wisdom—He knows our need for it, and He is willing to supply it. James assures us, *"It will be given to him."* Wisdom will be given to the one who asks God for it.

This passage also points to three primary reasons why we might not have the wisdom we require. First, we might not see our need for it, and therefore we don't acknowledge that we lack wisdom. We trust in ourselves and our own understanding (a trust that can lead to disaster). Second, we might realize we lack wisdom, but it doesn't occur to us to ask God for it. Third, we do not ask in faith. God insists that we ask, and also that we believe He will give us what we ask for. That is why James adds, *"But when he asks, he must believe and not doubt,"* which is consistent with the whole teaching of the Bible. For instance, we read in Hebrews:

He that cometh to God must believe that He is, and that He is a rewarder of them that diligently seek Him.

(Hebrews 11:6 KJV)

Accordingly, what does God require of us when we pray about anything? He requires that we believe in Him, and that we believe He will reward us with an answer. As James says,

When he asks, he must believe and not doubt, because he who doubts is like a wave of the sea, blown and tossed by the wind. That man should not think he will receive anything from the

Lord; he is a double-minded man, unstable in all he does.

(James 1:6–8 NIV)

That is a very strong statement. Men and women who are double-minded are unstable in everything they do, and they cannot expect to receive anything from the Lord. In seeking wisdom from God, therefore, we must set our hearts and minds to believe that if we ask in humble faith, He will give us what we ask for. He is waiting to give to us. In reality, He is waiting for us to see our need and ask Him to meet it.

FORSAKING FOOLISHNESS

To learn more about wisdom, it is helpful to take an honest look at the opposite of wisdom—foolishness. We need to understand that foolishness is not merely a lack of intelligence. There is a moral quality to it; it indicates a heart that is not in tune with God. In Mark 7:21–22, Jesus gives a list of evil traits that come out of the unregenerate human heart:

For from within, out of the heart of men, proceed the evil thoughts, fornications, thefts, murders, adulteries, deeds of coveting and wickedness, as well as deceit, sensuality, envy, slander, pride, and foolishness.   (NASB)

Notice what bad company foolishness keeps! It is linked with thefts, murders, adulteries, envy, slander, pride, and many other evil activities. Here is an interesting fact: in colloquial Arabic, the opposite of the word for "clever" is the word for "lazy." So again, there is a moral significance to foolishness. It indicates a lack of character.

ACCESSING WISDOM

Earlier, we answered the question "Where is wisdom?" We saw that Jesus Himself is the wisdom given to us by God. Since

Jesus Christ is the repository of wisdom from God, and "*all the treasures of wisdom and knowledge*" (Colossians 2:3 NIV) are found in Him, how do we access these treasures? How does God supply that for which we ask?

WALK IN FELLOWSHIP WITH THE HOLY SPIRIT

One primary answer to these questions is found in the book of John, where Jesus is speaking to His disciples about the work of the Holy Spirit:

> *But when He, the Spirit of truth, comes, He will guide you into all the truth; for He will not speak on His own initiative, but whatever He hears, He will speak; and He will disclose to you what is to come. He shall glorify Me; for He shall take of Mine, and shall disclose it to you. All things that the Father has are Mine; therefore I said, that He takes of Mine, and will disclose it to you.* (John 16:13–15 NASB)

It is clear from all we have learned so far that the treasures of wisdom and knowledge are in Christ. But the One who makes these treasures available to us is the Holy Spirit, who discloses them to us. The Holy Spirit is the Administrator of the riches of the kingdom of God, including "*all the treasures of wisdom and knowledge*" (Colossians 2:3 NIV) found in Christ.

In order to receive the wisdom God has promised to give us, we must therefore have an ongoing, close, and personal relationship with the Holy Spirit. We must walk in harmony and in fellowship with God's Spirit. We must also be able to hear what the Spirit is saying by being sensitive to His gentle nudges, and we must give heed to the warnings He provides us.

So many times, we get into trouble because we run through one of the red lights the Holy Spirit has put up in our way. When we ignore His warnings, we inevitably end up in some kind of accident or problem. Such misfortunes do not happen because wisdom was not available to us. Rather, they happen because we disregarded the wisdom the Holy Spirit gave us.

In Romans 8:14, Paul writes, *"For all who are being led by the Spirit of God, these are sons of God"* (NASB). In this verse, the Greek word translated *"sons"* indicates maturity. The mark of the mature believer is to be continually led by the Holy Spirit. That maturity causes us to be sensitive to every little nudge, every word of direction, and every whisper of the Spirit. If we operate in this way, wisdom will continually be made available to us.

FEED ON GOD'S WRITTEN WISDOM

Let me offer one more practical suggestion for how to receive wisdom: *feed your mind on God's written provision for wisdom in His Word.* The book of Proverbs is one of the greatest books on wisdom. The first chapter opens with these statements:

> [These proverbs are] *for attaining wisdom and discipline; for understanding words of insight; for acquiring a disciplined and prudent life, doing what is right and just and fair; for giving prudence to the simple, knowledge and discretion to the young.* (Proverbs 1:2–4 NIV)

May I put before you a personal challenge? There are thirty-one chapters in Proverbs. Why not read one chapter each day, and do that every month for a year? I can assure you that at the end of that time, you will be much wiser than you were at the beginning of the year!

PRAYING FOR WISDOM

Perhaps you are currently seeking God's wisdom—and you know how badly you need it. Maybe, as you have read through this chapter, you have sensed an inner longing for a deeper, more intimate relationship with the Holy Spirit—the One who makes the treasures of wisdom found in Christ available to us. I encourage you to express these desires to the Lord now through the following prayer:

> Father, I come to You today seeking and asking for the wisdom I have just read about. I proclaim my belief in You, and I affirm the truth that You are a rewarder of those who diligently seek You.
>
> I ask that You will help me to access the treasures of wisdom hidden in Jesus Christ. I also ask for a more intimate walk with Your Holy Spirit, one that is deeper than I have known up to now. Thank You for Your loving-kindness and faithfulness to me. You know what I lack and what I need. Thank You, Lord, for making Your wisdom available to me through the power of the Holy Spirit. Amen.

In our next chapter, we will focus on one particular promise of God closely related to wisdom—the promise of guidance.

INHERITING THE BLESSINGS

But by His [God's] doing you are in Christ Jesus, who became to us wisdom from God, and righteousness and sanctification, and redemption.   (1 Corinthians 1:30 NASB)

If any of you lacks wisdom, he should ask God, who gives generously to all without finding fault, and it will be given to him. But when he asks, he must believe and not doubt, because he who doubts is like a wave of the sea, blown and tossed by the wind. That man should not think he will receive anything from the Lord; he is a double-minded man, unstable in all he does.   (James 1:5–8 NIV)

17

LIFELONG GUIDANCE

For the last few chapters, we have identified certain needs and problems that commonly arise in our lives. Then we have considered practical ways those needs can be met and those problems can be solved, by applying specific promises in God's Word that correspond to them. The focus of our preceding chapter was one of God's choicest promises to us: access, through Christ, to all the treasures of wisdom, which we so clearly need for every aspect of our lives.

When we seek wisdom, it is often related to a search for *guidance*. This search encompasses the question of *how to find the right way in each situation and circumstance of our lives*. In this chapter, we will explore promises of God in our inheritance that deal with guidance—the need for practical direction in any given situation.

TWO KINDS OF GUIDANCE

First, we must establish a general principle that applies to many situations we will face over the course of our lives. It will help us to understand how God makes wisdom and guidance available to us. God provides two forms of guidance. The first is *general guidance*, which is applicable for all of God's people. The second is *individual guidance*, which applies only to a certain person in a particular situation.

General guidance comes from Scripture, a truth that is emphasized in the Bible again and again. One example is Psalm 119:105: "*Thy word is a lamp unto my feet, and a light unto my path*" (KJV). According to this promise, if we want to walk in God's ways, the source of light that shows us how to put our feet in the right place is the Word of God. It is an absolute principle that all other guidance must be tested against God's Word. John Wesley said, in effect, "I acknowledge no other rule of faith or practice but the Holy Scriptures."

No other rule of faith or practice has the same authority as the Holy Scriptures. Indeed, we must walk in the light of the Scriptures—because they are the primary source of guidance from God for all of His people. Furthermore, only when we are obedient to the general guidance of Scripture do we have the right to expect individual guidance.

THE DESIRES OF YOUR HEART

Let us now consider some specific promises in Scripture about guidance. The first is found in Psalm 37:4:

> *Delight yourself in the* LORD; *and He will give you the desires*
> *of your heart.* (NASB)

In the first part of this verse, we see a depiction of the kind of people who qualify for receiving the promise that is stated in the second part of the verse. Let us look at it again. David, the author of this psalm, said, "*Delight yourself in the* LORD; *and He will give you the desires of your heart.*"

When I was a young believer, this is how I understood the meaning of this verse: *If I take pleasure in God and do what God wants, then He will give me all that I want to do or to enjoy.* However, as I became more mature, I saw that the promise goes much deeper. If I delight myself in the Lord—if I really seek to please the Lord and find my satisfaction in Him—then He will give me the desires of my heart. However, it will be in this sense: *through the Holy Spirit, God will implant in my heart the desires that He wants to fulfill.* Consequently, my desires will change. They will become godly and God-pleasing rather than self-centered and self-pleasing.

If we delight ourselves in the Lord, it will lead to a transformation of our desires, our motives, and our ambitions. Instead of being selfish and self-focused, we will receive from God, by the Holy Spirit, desires, motives, and ambitions that are God-focused. By our positive response to those desires, and as we fulfill those ambitions, God will glorify Himself and extend His kingdom. Therefore, to claim this promise, you and I must become the kind of people who delight ourselves in the Lord in such a way that He implants in our hearts the desires He Himself intends to fulfill. Let me add that those desires are much better and more profitable for us. They will do us more good than our own selfish desires and ambitions, which are often harmful to us.

A PROMISE IN THREE PHASES

The kind of people who qualify for the promise of receiving the desires of their hearts also qualify for the promise that follows in the next verse:

> Commit your way to the LORD, trust also in Him, and He
> will do it.   (Psalm 37:5 NASB)

1. COMMIT YOUR WAY TO THE LORD

In this Scripture, there are three successive phases. The first phase is an *act*: "*Commit your way to the LORD.*" Committing is a single act, and it is performed just once. Interestingly enough, the original Hebrew literally means, "Roll your way on the Lord." What do you think the psalmist meant by that?

I have my own particular answer to that question, based on a personal experience I had when I was the principal of a college in East Africa for training African teachers. It would be helpful for you to know, first of all, that the principal of the college was considered to be everybody's servant. He had to do everything. If a tap leaked, he had to fix it. If there was a food shortage, he somehow had to come up with the needed provisions. That was one of the tasks I often had to perform; I would drive down into the local city and collect food for our students. Since one of their favorite foods was rice, I would collect big sacks of rice, each of which weighed 112 pounds! Then, with these huge bags of rice loaded into my little station wagon, I would pull up to the door of the storehouse where the food was kept.

I had been trying to find ways to impress upon the students enrolled at the school that it was not undignified for an educated person to work with his hands. The students often developed the attitude that because they had been to secondary school and college, it was now beneath their dignity to do manual labor. Therefore, I would try to set an example for them by helping to unload those very heavy sacks of rice from the back of the station wagon.

I found that if the sack of rice was standing upright in the back of the station wagon, it was not difficult to get it up on my back and carry it into the storehouse. However, the difficult part was getting it off my back again. In fact, with any wrong movement, I could easily have injured my back. I discovered that instead of removing the sack rather slowly, I could give a little, quick jerk and roll the sack off my back in one movement, so that it stood up on its end on the floor beside me.

In so doing, I saw why the psalmist says to "roll your way on the Lord," or "roll your burden on the Lord." You see, making our way through life is like carrying a 112-pound sack of rice. It is too heavy for us to handle by ourselves; the decisions and responsibilities are too great. The psalmist instructs, "Don't try to carry that sack. Just roll it off your back and leave it at the Lord's feet—and He'll take care of it."

2. TRUST IN GOD

The second phase indicated in the above verse is an attitude: *trust*. "*Trust also in Him.*" Committing is a one-time act, but trusting is an ongoing outlook. Once we have committed, we do not go on repeating that process over and over again. We adopt the attitude that our situation has once and for all been entrusted to the Lord. From then on, all we must do is continue trusting. Committing is the act; trusting is the attitude.

3. LET GOD DO IT

The third phase from the verse is something we leave to God: "[God] *will do it.*" The original Hebrew literally means, "God *is doing* it." I understand the progression in this way: First, we commit our way to the Lord. Second, we maintain an attitude of steady, continuing trust. At this point, the matter is in God's hands, and as long as we continue trusting, God is doing it. In other words, He is working out whatever we have committed to Him. Whatever decision we make and whatever course we need to take, God is working it out.

To me, this process is a lot like depositing money in a savings account. The initial deposit of the money is the act of commitment. Once you have made the deposit, it is not necessary to keep running back to the bank every day, checking to see if your money is bearing interest. You just *know* that the bank is regularly adding the interest to your money. That is an attitude of continuing trust. As long as your leave your money safely deposited in the bank, you can confidently maintain an attitude of trust that the bank is managing the money in your savings account. It is the same with God. "Commit your way to Him, trust in Him, and He is doing it."

GOD WILL MAKE THE RIGHT WAY

Let's consider another promise of direction from the Lord, from the book of Proverbs:

> Trust in the LORD with all your heart and lean not on your own understanding; in all your ways acknowledge Him, and He will make your paths straight.   (Proverbs 3:5–6 NIV)

I would like to point out one alternate translation for the end of this verse, from the *New King James Version*: "*...and He shall direct your paths.*" God will direct us in the right way through life. This is His promise of the guidance we need for any given, present situation.

There are three conditions for the fulfillment of this promise, which are similar to the conditions in Psalm 37. Let's take a moment to examine them one by one. The first condition is "*Trust in the LORD with all your heart.*" You will find that if you maintain a continuing attitude of trust in God, it will always be accompanied by peace. If you become fretful and anxious, those attitudes are a fairly certain indication that you have stopped trusting.

The second condition is negative: "*Lean not on your own understanding.*" Do not go back to trusting your own judgment and trying to work out situations yourself. This is actually one of the greatest hindrances to receiving answers to prayer from God. In so many cases, we pray—but then we try to work out how God should answer our prayer. We need to acknowledge that God is not committed to answering our prayer the way we might think. Furthermore, when we are trying to work things out for ourselves, we have fallen into a faulty attitude that makes it difficult for us to receive the answer God is working out on our behalf. For all these reasons, we must not lean on our own understanding.

The third condition is, "*In all your ways acknowledge Him.*" What does that mean? Let me explain the way I understand the idea of "acknowledging God in all your ways." At any given moment, in any given situation, and at any given time or place, acknowledging God means to stop and say, "Lord, I thank You for Your faithfulness to me. I thank You for all the good You've already done for me. I thank You for the way You have proved Yourself in so many situations and circumstances in my life. You've brought me this far—and I trust You to continue to lead me." That is how to acknowledge God in all your ways.

GOD WILL DIRECT YOUR PATHS

In 1964, I resigned from a rather secure pastorate in a city in the Pacific Northwest. I had committed myself to become an itinerant minister, without any fixed salary or any permanent place of abode. I had no capital—not even a car of my own. I had a wife and child to support, yet I knew that God was thrusting me out into this new ministry. As I was waiting upon God and seeking Him for some form of security in this new situation, the Lord gave me the Scripture we have been examining: "*In all thy ways acknowledge Him, and He shall direct thy paths*" (Proverbs 3:6 KJV).

I want to testify that I have proved this beautiful Scripture to be true throughout all the intervening years. I can highly recommend that every time you come to a turning point in your life, the best practice is to pause and begin to acknowledge God. Thank Him for all He has already done for you, for all His faithfulness, for the way He has answered so many prayers and solved so many problems in the past. Then, having acknowledged Him, go on trusting Him to be as faithful in the future as He has been in the past, knowing that He will direct your paths.

Taking a moment right now to acknowledge God would be a wonderful way to end this chapter. Would you like to join with me in this prayer of acknowledgement?

Lord, You have been so good to me—far beyond anything I could ever have asked for or deserved. You have been faithful every step of the way—guiding me, helping me, and providing for me.

You have helped me through the challenges and difficulties I have faced so far, and I know and trust that Your help will continue. Thank You for Your love and faithfulness toward me.

I agree with the psalmist by declaring, "In all my ways, I acknowledge You." I know You will continue to direct my paths. For all of this, dear Lord, I give You praise and thanks. In Jesus's name, amen.

INHERITING THE BLESSINGS

Delight yourself in the LORD; and He will give you the desires of your heart. Commit your way to the LORD, trust also in Him, and He will do it.   (Psalm 37:4–5 NASB)

Trust in the LORD with all your heart and lean not on your own understanding; in all your ways acknowledge Him, and He will make your paths straight.   (Proverbs 3:5–6 NIV)

18

FAVOR IN
THE WORKPLACE

God has clearly promised to give wisdom to His people wherever and whenever they need it. A particular form of wisdom God provides is His *guidance*, through which He shows us how to find the right way in each situation and circumstance of our lives. In this chapter, we take these wisdom principles to the workplace—an area where the practical need for guidance is daily experienced by many Christians in the world today.

PROMISES REGARDING OPPOSITION AND PERSECUTION

Most committed Christians who seek to lead lives of righteousness that glorify their Lord will experience some degree of strain or tension in their work situations. Often, they are working with fellow employees or under employers who are not believers, some of whom may even be hostile to the Christian faith. In some cases, they may actually face daily opposition or even persecution.

Does the Bible have any guidance for Christians who find themselves in such circumstances? Based on my own experiences,

I believe it does. In this connection, let me share some of the promises I have relied on during my years of walking with the Lord in the land of His promises.

The first promise we will consider is one most of us would rather not need to access if we had the choice. Nevertheless, it is part of the array of promises from God's Word, and we must give heed to it. Second Timothy 3:12 says, *"And indeed, all who desire to live godly in Christ Jesus will be persecuted"* (NASB).

Those words constitute a promise! You might say, "Well, it's not a very pleasant promise!" However, it is part of our total inheritance. Remember, our inheritance is *all* the promises of God—both the ones we like and the ones we might not like. We cannot separate one from the other and say, "Well, I'll take the pleasant promises, but I don't want the unpleasant ones." It is important to understand that they all go together. Why? Because when we are in a situation where we are being persecuted for living in a genuinely godly way, it is very comforting to know that such treatment is part of our inheritance.

By His grace, God has made provision for such circumstances because He understands they will happen. These occurrences do not signify that we are doing something wrong in our lives or that we are out of the will of God. Facing difficulties and persecution is part of the Christian life. Remember, we are coheirs not only of Christ's blessings but also of His sufferings.

The Word of God does not promise that you will never be persecuted. In fact, on the basis of Scripture, I can clearly suggest that if you truly live a godly life in Christ Jesus, there will be times when you *will* be persecuted for it. Nevertheless, I believe God has certain answers to such situations, which He works out in us, both for His glory and for our good.

BIBLICAL STANDARDS AND QUALITIES FOR EMPLOYEES

First, we need to identify certain biblical qualities and standards of conduct for employees, which the New Testament clearly establishes in Ephesians 6:5–7. Although this instruction is addressed to "*slaves,*" for today's society, we could substitute the term *servants* or *employees*. (Of course, the conditions faced by slaves in the first century were often far more abusive than those faced by modern employees. Yet no matter what level of service is involved, the same admonitions apply.) This is what the New Testament says to employees or servants:

> *Slaves* [employees], *obey your earthly masters with respect and fear, and with sincerity of heart, just as you would obey Christ. Obey them not only to win their favor when their eye is on you, but like slaves of Christ, doing the will of God from your heart. Serve wholeheartedly, as if you were serving the Lord, not men.*   (Ephesians 6:5–7 NIV)

RESPECTFUL, SINCERE, WHOLEHEARTED

There are certain attitudes we are required to maintain in our conduct toward our employer, the one who has authority over us. We are required to show respect, sincerity, and wholehearted service. The principle behind this requirement is the following: in our given work situation and position, our employer, or our supervisor, is God's representative to us. We must see that person as the one whom God has placed over us in that particular place and time.

If we show no respect for our employer—if we cheat, serve short hours, or give shoddy service—that is really a reflection of our attitude toward God. We might not dare to show such behavior openly toward Him. But the response and effort we give to our employer or supervisor is, in fact, an indication of our true heart attitude toward the Lord. Once we realize this reality, it will help to transform us into the kind of employees that employers will be happy to have working for them.

TRUSTWORTHY

The next quality we need to recognize is faithfulness or trustworthiness. Proverbs 20:6 says,

> *Many a man proclaims his own loyalty, but who can find a trustworthy man?* (NASB)

That proverb was true about three thousand years ago when this passage was written—and I would say it is even truer today. I am an employer myself, and I have many friends who are businessmen. I often find myself moving in business circles, and I would say the question many employers regularly ask today is, "Who can find a trustworthy man or woman?" Too often, such people are hard to find. The whole trend of modern society is toward indiscipline and irresponsibility. As a result, it is becoming harder and harder to find employees who are truly trustworthy.

My conviction is that people in any employed positions who truly prove they are trustworthy will, in due course, be appreciated and approved by their employers. It may take time, but as they prove their trustworthiness, they will be valued. Proverbs 28:20 contains this observation:

> *A faithful man will be richly blessed, but one eager to get rich will not go unpunished.* (NIV)

If you are a faithful man or woman in your place of employment and in your attitude toward your employer, God says you will be blessed. Even if your employer does not bless you, God—in His own way and time—will see to it that you are blessed.

"PLEASING TO GOD AND APPROVED BY MEN"

So far, we have looked at the negative promise, *"All who desire to live godly in Christ Jesus will be persecuted"* (2 Timothy 3:12 NASB), and we have examined some of the standards the Bible sets for employees. Now let's turn to the positive promise:

> *For the kingdom of God is not a matter of eating and drinking, but of righteousness, peace and joy in the Holy Spirit, because anyone who serves Christ in this way is pleasing to God and approved by men.*   (Romans 14:17–18 NIV)

Please notice what the kingdom of God is *not*. It is not a set of legalistic, religious rules about, for example, what to eat, what to drink, or what places of entertainment to attend. This isn't how the kingdom of God is manifested. As a matter of fact, I find that such types of religious legalism tend to turn off people who are not Christians. Religious rules do not attract them—they repel them. The real life of Christianity is *"righteousness, peace and joy in the Holy Spirit."* Apart from the Holy Spirit, a joyous Christian life is not possible.

What does Paul say about the person who is serving God in righteousness, peace, and joy in the Holy Spirit? That individual is *"pleasing to God and approved by men."* If you serve God in that way, others around you will recognize the quality of your life. They will grant you their approval, even if it is grudgingly given.

I can honestly say that I have proved this in my own experience. As I wrote earlier, in World War II, I was a soldier in the British Army. After I had been in the army for less than a year, I experienced a wonderful conversion to Jesus Christ. My whole life was instantly, radically, and permanently changed. As a result, my fellow soldiers simply could not understand the transformation they saw in me. At first, they would say, "He's become religious," and I would correct them and say, "No, it's not religion; I've been saved." They did not understand what that meant, but they genuinely disliked it.

However, God gave me grace to lead the kind of life that was consistent with what I was saying about my experience. After a while, I noticed that I had begun to earn their respect. One lesson I learned was never to compromise my faith at the beginning of a new situation. For instance, if I was moved into a new room in the barracks, the first night, I would deliberately kneel down by my bed and say my prayers. It's not that I thought it was essential to pray kneeling down, but I just wanted to let everybody in that barracks room know where I stood. Even though, at first, my fellow soldiers exhibited a kind of coolness and hesitation toward me, in the end, I found that those men respected me.

Later, this respect became obvious, especially on occasions when we were in dangerous circumstances in the North African desert. For example, one time our company was cut off behind enemy lines, which is something that easily happens in desert warfare. In the midst of such dangerous times, some of these ungodly, blaspheming men came to me privately and said, "Corporal Prince, I'm glad you're with us." In other words, they felt I was a kind of insurance policy for them. They knew God was with me. And if God was with me, then somehow it would rub off on them. As a matter of fact, remarkably, it did. Our company had an extraordinary record of safety and protection during the period I was with those men in the desert.

A CONFIRMING PROMISE

My experience during World War II is a simple example of how serving God with the right attitude in every situation can gain you the approval of other people, even if they do not want to join you in your faith. The same principle is stated elsewhere in the Bible. The third chapter of Proverbs says:

> *My son, do not forget my teaching, but keep my commands in your heart…. Then you will win favor and a good name in the sight of God and man.*   (Proverbs 3:1, 4 NIV)

Favor with God and man is promised if we will walk in obedience to God's commandments. There are some outstanding examples of people in the history of the Bible who proved this promise to be true. Joseph was in jail in Egypt, but the Scripture says, for example, *"The LORD…gave him favor in the sight of the chief jailer"* (Genesis 39:21 NASB). Daniel was an exile in Babylon, but *"God granted Daniel favor and compassion in the sight of the commander of the officials"* (Daniel 1:9 NASB). No matter where you are, if you walk uprightly with God and please Him, He will give you favor with man. One of the most practical areas where we can see this promise fulfilled for us is in the marketplace.

INHERITING THE BLESSINGS

> *For the kingdom of God is not a matter of eating and drinking, but of righteousness, peace and joy in the Holy Spirit, because anyone who serves Christ in this way is pleasing to God and approved by men.*   (Romans 14:17–18 NIV)

> *My son, do not forget my teaching, but keep my commands in your heart…. Then you will win favor and a good name in the sight of God and man.*   (Proverbs 3:1, 4 NIV)

19

FINDING THE RIGHT SPOUSE

On this journey through the land of God's promises, it is wonderful to discover what God has provided for each and every situation in our lives. And as part of our inheritance in Christ, there are promises in God's Word that relate to one of the most important decisions a man or a woman must ever make: the choice of a wife or a husband.

In a previous chapter, we talked about how God provides us with two kinds of guidance: *general guidance*, which is applicable for all of God's people, and *individual guidance*, which applies only to a certain person in a particular situation. With this perspective in mind, let us look at some principles of general guidance in Scripture with regard to marriage.

GOD'S PURPOSES AND PROVISIONS FOR MARRIAGE

THE CREATION STANDARD

First, let us examine the standard for marriage Jesus acknowledged, and which He set for His disciples. This standard is brought out very clearly in the book of Matthew, which records a conversation between Jesus and some Pharisees who came to Him about the question of marriage and divorce.

> *And some Pharisees came to Him, testing Him, and saying, "Is it lawful for a man to divorce his wife for any cause at all?" And He answered and said, "Have you not read, that He who created them from the beginning made them male and female, and said, 'For this cause a man shall leave his father and mother, and shall cleave to his wife; and the two shall become one flesh'? Consequently they are no longer two, but one flesh. What therefore God has joined together, let no man separate."* (Matthew 19:3–6 NASB)

It is very important to see that when Jesus was questioned about marriage, He did not accept the standards, rules, or conventions of the time in which He lived. Instead, He went back to God's original purpose and standard for marriage when He first created man and woman, as recorded in Genesis. That is the only standard and purpose of marriage Jesus accepted as valid. What does that mean for us as His disciples? If we are to follow God's provisions for marriage in our lives, we, too, must go back to His purpose and standard at creation.

FOUR FACTS FOR TODAY

In connection with this original standard, there are four facts about Adam and Eve from Genesis 2 that I believe are applicable for our lives today.

1. It was God who decided that Adam needed a wife. (See verse 18.)

2. It was God who formed Eve for Adam. (See verses 21–22.)

3. It was God who presented Eve to Adam. (See verse 22.)

4. It was God who determined the nature of their relationship. (See verses 23–24.)

Here is how these principles apply to both men and women today. First, for men:

+ God will decide whether you need a wife. It is not your decision; it is His.

+ God will form the right wife for you.

+ God will bring your wife to you.

+ God will determine the nature of the relationship in which you will live as a married couple.

If you are a woman, the same principles are applicable, but in a somewhat different way:

+ God will decide that a certain man needs you as his wife.

+ God will form you and prepare you to be a wife for that man.

+ God will bring you to that man.

+ God will determine the nature of the relationship in which you will live as a married couple.

Whether you are a man or a woman, the initiative, the decision, and the process of preparation are all God's.

FINDING FAVOR

A related general principle from God's Word is that *God appoints the right mate for each one of His believing children.* Finding the right mate is not a random process—and it is not outside of God's provision. Proverbs 18:22 tells us how important the choice of our mate is to God:

He who finds a wife finds a good thing, and obtains favor from the LORD. (NASB)

In other words, finding the right wife is an indication of the Lord's favor. This idea is confirmed for us in Proverbs 19:14:

Houses and wealth are inherited from parents, but a prudent wife is from the LORD. (NIV)

Therefore, if you are a man and desire to have a prudent wife, you need to seek the Lord about it. Personally, I can say a double "amen" to both the above Scriptures. It has been my privilege in life to be married twice. On each occasion—as a single man and as a widower—it was the Lord who very definitely directed me to the right mate. In both marriages, the Lord provided me with a prudent wife, a blessing for which I cannot possibly ever thank Him too much. Let me add that, in both cases, I was not so much seeking to be married as I was concerned about fulfilling God's plan for my life. In each situation, He foresaw my need for a prudent wife. I believe that because my heart was set on doing His will, He brought the right spouses to me.

AVOIDING AN UNEVEN YOKE

I want to emphasize a third general principle about marriage. Here it is very simply: *It is wrong for a believer to marry an unbeliever.* Many of God's people seem to be somewhat foggy about this principle, yet it is stated very clearly by Paul in 2 Corinthians 6:14–16:

Do not be yoked together with unbelievers. For what do righteousness and wickedness have in common? Or what fellowship can light have with darkness? What harmony is there between Christ and Belial? What does a believer have in common with an unbeliever? What agreement is there between the temple of God and idols? For we are the temple of the living God. (NIV)

In this passage, Paul is writing to believers, and in Scripture, marriage is commonly referred to as a "yoke." Notice the very pertinent questions raised here: *"What do righteousness and wickedness have in common?"* *"What fellowship can light have with darkness?"* Believers are light, and light cannot have fellowship with the darkness of unbelief.

Therefore, if you are an *unmarried* believer, you ought not to seek a life mate who is not a believer. On the other hand, if you were married as an unbeliever and later came to believe in the Lord, that is a different situation. In that circumstance, you can trust the Lord to come to your help in various ways. But at the present time, we are dealing with the choice of a life partner for one who is not married.

WHAT DOES GOD REQUIRE?

Let's close this chapter by addressing a very practical question: What does God require of me to find the mate He has chosen for me? I want to give you seven simple guidelines that I believe will greatly help you in this matter.

1. *Believe in God's purpose for your life.* Believe God has a destiny for you. You are not just an accident looking for a place to happen. God has a purpose for you—and it is a *good purpose.*

2. *Commit your life totally to God.* Hold nothing back from Him. Without reservation, seek obedience to His will in everything.

3. *Walk in the light of God's Word.* Live according to the general guidance God has made available in Scripture to all His people.

4. *Cultivate fellowship with God's people.* It may be that God has chosen the person you are going to marry from the people with whom you fellowship. Remember, if you fellowship primarily with unbelievers, you are likely to end up marrying an unbeliever.

5. *Realize your value as a child of God.* Do not cheapen yourself by accepting second best in this vital matter of marriage. The trouble with many Christians is that they do not place sufficient value upon themselves. They do not regard themselves highly enough as children of God, and consequently they accept some poor substitute for God's best.

6. *Be prepared to wait.* Waiting is one evidence of faith—and God often requires us to demonstrate our willingness to trust Him.

7. *Be sensitive to the Holy Spirit.* Let Him choose—let Him direct you. If you listen to Him and obey Him, He will always lead you in the way that is most beneficial to you.

A PRAYER FOR YOUR MATE

Would you like to take a moment to commit yourself in prayer to this process of selecting a spouse? Even if you are already married, there may be some benefit in using these principles to make a renewed commitment to your mate in prayer. Let's pray together, incorporating the above seven principles.

Lord, I believe You have a purpose for my life, and I commit myself totally to You. I commit myself now to walk in the light of Your Word and to cultivate fellowship with Your people.

I proclaim that I am Your child—someone upon whom You have placed great value.

Help me, Lord, to be willing to wait patiently and faithfully for Your choice of my life partner. Help me to be sensitive to the leading and direction of Your Holy Spirit as You guide me into the future You have destined for me. Amen.

INHERITING THE BLESSINGS

Then the L*ORD* *God said, "It is not good for the man to be alone; I will make him a helper suitable for him."*
(Genesis 2:18 NASB)

He who finds a wife finds a good thing, and obtains favor from the L*ORD.* (Proverbs 18:22 NASB)

Houses and wealth are inherited from parents, but a prudent wife is from the L*ORD.* (Proverbs 19:14 NIV)

20

DEALING WITH PROBLEM CHILDREN

In the previous chapter, we looked at God's provision for marriage. It is natural to assume that most marriages will include children. Although a family is a blessing from God, unfortunately, in any family situation, difficulties can often arise. In many families today, parents are dealing with what are commonly referred to as "problem children." Does the Word of God offer us direction and encouragement in this, one of the most difficult and painful situations we can encounter? I believe it does. Let's look at some significant promises in this regard.

THE GREATEST SOCIAL ISSUE OF OUR DAY

The first Scripture passage we will consider is from the prophet Malachi, the last prophet of the Old Testament. This passage is a portrayal of a scene that will be fulfilled at some point before the tremendous climax of the close of this age—the time period in which I believe we are living today. In Malachi 4:5–6, the Lord says:

> *See, I will send you the prophet Elijah before that great and dreadful day of the LORD comes. He will turn the hearts of the*

*fathers to their children, and the hearts of the children to their
fathers; or else I will come and strike the land with a curse.*

(NIV)

This prophecy cites the problem of wrong relationships within
the family, especially between fathers and their children. With
great prophetic insight, the Word of God accurately pinpoints the
greatest single social issue of our age: disrupted families caused
by disharmony between parents and children. The Lord also indicates that if these relationships are not adjusted, and the situation
is not changed, the result will be that the whole land will suffer
under a curse.

I am firmly convinced that this describes the situation in
America and many other nations today. It is our most pressing
issue—more pressing than military, political, or economic issues.
Thus, the greatest threat to our civilization is the problem in the
family—the disrupted homes that are the result of fathers, mothers, and children not functioning in right relationship with one
another.

Marriage and the family are the building stones of a healthy
culture. If they fail, a nation will cease to bring forth the kinds
of young people upon which a sound culture may be built for the
future. Unless we accept God's solution and turn back to Him in
line with the conditions He outlines, the result will be a curse. It
will settle upon any culture or nation where this problem prevails.

ROOT CAUSES

WRONG PRIORITIES

Please notice that in Malachi's prophecy, God places the primary obligation for healing the broken situation upon the fathers.
The Lord says He *"will turn the hearts of the fathers to their children, and the hearts of the children to their fathers"* (Malachi 4:6).

However, the hearts of the fathers *must turn first*. As a result, the children will turn back to their fathers. This is a logical sequence and is in accordance with the principles of God's Word, which teach that the primary responsibility for right order in a home is placed very clearly upon the fathers.

This does not mean that mothers have no responsibility. Indeed, they have a great responsibility to stand with their husbands and be the kind of wives and mothers the family needs. But the initial and primary responsibility for the order of the home and the family is placed by God upon the fathers. This is clearly stated in Ephesians 6:4:

> *Fathers, do not provoke your children to anger; but bring them up in the discipline and instruction of the Lord.*   (NASB)

The above verse highlights two primary duties of a father: *discipline* and *instruction*. The father is charged by God with maintaining order in the home through proper, loving discipline. At the same time, he is responsible to give his children instruction in the ways of the Lord from the principles of Scripture. He is to train them in right living in the Christian faith.

Looking at American fathers, I would have to say that most of them have failed to follow God's instructions. They are not providing the discipline and instruction their families need. I have dealt with countless numbers of cases in which the root problem in the life of the person I was ministering to was the failure of the parents in the home.

In my opinion, the reason why most American fathers have failed in the past—and are still failing today—is that they have neglected to establish right priorities. They do not value their homes and their children as highly as they should. They put other concerns first: success in business, making money, keeping up a high standard of living, and entertainment. They allow too many other pursuits to take priority over that most valuable and wonderful gift God has given to them—their children. Consequently, they do not fulfill their duties and responsibilities toward them.

DISHARMONY BETWEEN THE PARENTS

Another major factor in this problem within families today is disharmony between the parents. James 3:16 tells us,

> For where you have envy and selfish ambition, there you find disorder and every evil practice.   (NIV)

Where there is envy or competitiveness between a husband and his wife, where each is guilty of selfish ambition, there will be "*disorder and every evil practice.*" It has been my observation that children who grow up in this kind of atmosphere are bound to have serious emotional and personal problems. In most cases, the issues of the parents go back to their own childhoods, where there was probably disharmony and inadequate parenting as well.

One of the other detriments stemming from a wrong relationship between a husband and wife is the hindrance of their prayers. The apostle Peter writes,

> Husbands, in the same way be considerate as you live with your wives, and treat them with respect as the weaker partner and as heirs with you of the gracious gift of life, so that nothing will hinder your prayers.   (1 Peter 3:7 NIV)

This Scripture makes it clear that a wrong relationship between husband and wife hinders their prayers in general. The result is bad enough in itself, but hindrance in prayer, by extension, will also inevitably affect the children in the family. On the other hand, Jesus told us that if two people can agree and harmonize together, anything they pray for will be granted. (See Matthew 18:19.) What two people should be better able to agree and harmonize together than a husband and wife? When they can agree together, the resulting atmosphere of harmony will permeate their homes, and their prayers on behalf of their children will be answered by God.

WHAT IS THE REMEDY?

What, then, is the answer to the breakdown in the family? I want to suggest three biblical steps parents need to take.

First of all, each parent should repent before God for his or her failure, in any respect, in relationship with the other partner and with the children. Repentance opens the way for the restoration of God's blessings.

Second, if there is disharmony between the parents, they need to make it their goal to be reconciled with each other. This will open the way for their prayers for their children to be answered—because, as 1 Peter 3:7 points out, their wrong relationship hinders their prayers.

Third, if parents have seriously failed their children in their parental duties, they need to humble themselves, go to their children, acknowledge their failure, and *ask for their forgiveness.* As a parent, I have had to take this step in my own family. More than once, I have had to go to one of my children and say, "I'm sorry. I was wrong. Please forgive me." Every time I have done so, my repentance has opened up the way for the restoration of a good relationship and God's blessing.

A LEGACY OF BLESSING

Once we have taken these steps, we qualify for the blessings contained in our salvation. Remember that *salvation* is an all-inclusive term that covers all the benefits provided for us through the death of Jesus Christ on the cross. It includes spiritual, physical, and material benefits in this life and in the next—in time and in eternity. These blessings include the well-being of our children. There are many promises about children in the Scriptures that are part of our inheritance. Here are two pertinent verses from Psalm 103:

> *But from everlasting to everlasting the* LORD'*s love is with those who fear Him, and His righteousness with their children's children—with those who keep His covenant and remember to obey His precepts.*   (Psalm 103:17–18 NIV)

This is a promise to those who keep God's covenant and remember to obey His precepts. One part of the promise is that God's righteousness is with their children's children. Not merely the next generation, but also the following generation, will be included in the blessings of God's righteousness.

When we are diligently keeping God's covenant and obeying His precepts, we have the right to expect that the Lord will pour out His blessings upon our families. We can trust that His righteousness will descend to our children and our children's children.

A similar promise is found in Psalm 112:1–2:

> *Blessed is the man who fears the* LORD, *who finds great delight in His commands. His children will be mighty in the land; the generation of the upright will be blessed.*   (NIV)

This is another clear promise that if our ways are pleasing to God, our descendants will be blessed. Additionally, we find promises for the restoration of our children in Isaiah 49:24–25:

> *Can plunder be taken from warriors, or captives rescued from the fierce? But this is what the* LORD *says: "Yes, captives will be taken from warriors, and plunder retrieved from the fierce; I will contend with those who contend with you, and your children I will save."*   (NIV)

The forces of evil—Satan and all of his invading armies—have moved into many of our homes. In essence, those forces have captured our children, taking them from us. This abduction may have occurred through drug use, illicit sex, the occult, or one of several forms of evil and deception. All of this can be the equivalent of an invasion by an evil army. However, God's promise is, "*'I will contend with those who contend with you, and your children I will save';* they will be delivered and retrieved from their fierce captors."

Finally, Jeremiah 31:15–17 offers a beautiful promise for mothers:

> *Thus says the* LORD, *"A voice is heard in Ramah, lamentation and bitter weeping. Rachel is weeping for her children; she refuses to be comforted for her children, because they are no more." Thus says the* LORD, *"Restrain your voice from weeping, and your eyes from tears; for your work shall be rewarded,"* declares the LORD, *"and they* [your children] *shall return from the land of the enemy. And there is hope for your future,"* declares the LORD, *"and your children shall return to their own territory."*   (NASB)

This is a promise for believing mothers who pray for their children. If you will hold on in faith to what God has promised, He will answer your prayers. I have seen God do this many, many times.

A PRAYER FOR OUR CHILDREN

Perhaps the topic of this chapter has touched you, and you recognize that as a parent, you need to take some restorative steps. Obviously, there may be an ongoing need for you to take the practical steps outlined earlier—a long-term process that will ultimately lead to the restoration of your children. But let's take some initiative now—a bold proclamation based upon the verses we have just reviewed from the Psalms, Isaiah, and Jeremiah:

Heavenly Father, I commit myself to keep Your covenant and obey Your precepts in the fear of the Lord. As I do so, Your love will be with me, and Your righteousness will be with my children and their children.

Lord, I further commit myself to fear You and to delight in Your commands. As I walk in this commitment, my children will be mighty in the land, and each succeeding generation of my family will be blessed.

Lord, concerning the fierce enemies that have taken my children captive, I declare that my children will be rescued and retrieved from these enemies. You Yourself will contend with those who oppose us, and You will save my children.

Lord, I will refrain from weeping, and I will dry my tears, because my work will be rewarded, and my children will return from the land of the enemy. You have spoken hope for our future, and my children will return to their own territory—their destiny in You. Amen.

INHERITING THE BLESSINGS

But from everlasting to everlasting the LORD's love is with those who fear Him, and His righteousness with their children's children—with those who keep His covenant and remember to obey His precepts.   (Psalm 103:17–18 NIV)

Can plunder be taken from warriors, or captives rescued from the fierce? But this is what the LORD says: "Yes, captives will be taken from warriors, and plunder retrieved from the fierce; I will contend with those who contend with you, and your children I will save."   (Isaiah 49:24–25 NIV)

21

MATERIAL PROVISION, PART 1: THE BASIS OF PROSPERITY

We have been comparing our journey through the land of God's promises to the journey made by the children of Israel in the promised land under the leadership of Joshua. God gave Joshua a specific way to gain possession of that land: step-by-step, stage-by-stage, area-by-area. That process may be summed up by Joshua 1:3, where God says, *"Every place on which the sole of your foot treads, I have given it to you"* (NASB).

The process by which we enter into our inheritance in Christ is exactly the same. It is step-by-step, stage-by-stage, area-by-area, according to God's promises. As we place our foot upon each succeeding promise of God, we possess that much more of our inheritance.

FOUR PROMISES OF BLESSING

We have seen that the promises of God apply to every area of our lives—including the material realm. In this chapter, we will focus on a promise of prosperity and success that is all-inclusive in its application. As amazing as it may seem, this promise can be claimed anywhere, at any time, by anyone who will fulfill the clearly stated conditions.

The promise and its conditions for prosperity and success are systematically outlined in Psalm 1:1–3. In a certain sense, these three verses set the tone for the entire book of Psalms. Psalms is essentially a book of praise and thanks to God for the blessedness of being related to Him, knowing Him, and walking in His ways.

> *How blessed is the man who does not walk in the counsel of the wicked, nor stand in the path of sinners, nor sit in the seat of scoffers! But his delight is in the law of the* Lord, *and in His law he meditates day and night. And he will be like a tree firmly planted by streams of water, which yields its fruit in its season, and its leaf does not wither; and in whatever he does, he prospers.* (Psalm 1:1–3 NASB)

The promises in this passage are presented in four sections. As we examine each section, I will be using the word *man* in the same way the psalm does, because that is how it is written. However, these promises apply equally to men and women of every age, race, and culture.

1. PLANTED FIRMLY

The first section of this psalm states that the man who fulfills God's conditions will be like a tree *"firmly planted by streams of water"* (Psalm 1:3 NASB). *"Firmly planted"* indicates a tree whose roots go down so deep into the soil that it cannot be shaken or overthrown by winds or storms. This is a picture of a person who is strong and steadfast. He is not rattled by adversity or unfavorable circumstances; his roots go down so deep that such challenges do not shake or overthrow him.

This passage also states that his roots go down into soil that is adjacent to streams of water. The picture here is of a root system that always has access to water; the water is conveyed up through the roots, giving life and health to the whole tree. A person with such roots does not have to rely on sporadic, temporary rainfall, nor is he threatened by drought. Rather, he is in a place and in a relationship with streams of water that flow continually. His supply of water from these streams does not change with the climate or the season.

2. FRUITFUL

The second part of the picture is that this person is fruitful—he yields his fruit in season. (See Psalm 1:3.) God requires that you and I produce spiritual fruit in our lives. Jesus said, *"Every tree that does not produce good fruit will be cut down and thrown into the fire"* (Matthew 3:10 NIV).

3. FLOURISHING

The third aspect of the picture is that this person's leaf, or foliage, *"does not wither"* (Psalm 1:3 NASB). The leaves are the most visible part of a tree. I believe this picture indicates that such a man presents a picture of thriving. One look at him tells you he is flourishing. It can be seen in his eyes and in the way he carries himself—there is just an atmosphere of well-being about him.

4. PROSPEROUS

Finally, we come to the promise on which we want to focus in this chapter: *"In whatever he does, he prospers"* (Psalm 1:3 NASB). This person is so completely in line with God's Word and His purposes that everything he does carries the blessing of God upon it. He never knows recurring failure or continual frustration. What a beautiful picture—and what a beautiful promise!

FIVE CONDITIONS FOR PROSPERITY

Having reviewed the promises, we must now look at the conditions. Five conditions are stated in this psalm: three are negative—in the sense that they represent actions we should not take—and two are positive. However, so we can better grasp the principles, I will phrase all the headings for these conditions in a positive way.

1. FOLLOWING GOOD COUNSEL

The first condition is that such a person *"does not walk in the counsel of the wicked"* (Psalm 1:1 NASB). In other words, he does not get his advice and input from the wrong sources. He relies upon good counsel.

How can we best define *"the counsel of the wicked,"* which we are to avoid? I will suggest five words or phrases that could easily be associated with wicked counsel.

1. The counsel of the wicked is *unethical.* This would be input that leads us to treat other people in a wrong way. The advice and instruction of the Bible is "The Golden Rule"—that we treat others the way we want them to treat us. (See Matthew 7:12.)

2. The counsel of the wicked is *dishonest,* in that it leads to shady practices. For example, such advice would encourage you to fudge on your income tax returns, to be corrupt in the handling of money, or to misrepresent facts in a given situation.

3. The counsel of the wicked is *immoral,* in that it encourages us to act in ways that conflict with the moral laws of God. Advice of this type might be summed up as being contrary to the last six of the Ten Commandments.

4. The counsel of the wicked is *wrongly motivated,* because it is not centered on God and on a motivation to love, please, and glorify Him above all else.

5. The counsel of the wicked is *not in line with God's principles*—a characteristic that naturally follows as a consequence of the preceding four statements. It runs contrary to the principles that govern the universe. Therefore, it is ultimately doomed to failure.

2. LIVING A GODLY LIFESTYLE

The second negative condition is that such a man should not "*stand in the path of sinners*" (Psalm 1:1 NASB). How does one avoid such a path? It requires a deliberate choice to live according to a different lifestyle—to cultivate friendships different in nature from many of those around us. The righteous person does not "hang around" in wrong places. He does not get his inspiration from a worldly gathering of people who do not adhere to the principles of God's Word. He follows a godly way of life, and his close friends live by God's principles rather than by those of the world.

3. HAVING A PURE HEART AND MIND

The third negative condition is that he does not "*sit in the seat of scoffers*" (Psalm 1:1 NASB). To me, "*the seat of scoffers*" indicates an attitude of *determined cynicism*. All too often, this dark, skeptical view of life prevails today in the world of business, in institutions of higher learning, and in the media. I believe it is a sure path to frustration and failure. The opposite of a scoffer would be someone with a pure heart and mind who trusts God in all situations.

Notice that in these three negative aspects, there is a "slowing down" process. The man who succumbs to negative tendencies begins by walking, then slows to a stand, and finally ends up sitting. His position and his situation get worse and worse as he continues in these incorrect pursuits.

4. DELIGHTING IN THE LAW OF THE LORD

Having seen the negative conditions, we now want to consider the positive conditions, which are twofold. First of all, such a man "*delight[s]…in the law of the* LORD" (Psalm 1:2 NASB). He derives his pleasure from the Word of God and the revelation of God's truth. It would be helpful for us to understand the particular meaning of the word "*law*" in this passage (and in much of the Old Testament). The Hebrew word translated "*law*" is *Torah*.

We sometimes think of Torah, or the Law, as just a set of rules. But it is much more than that. The root meaning of the word is "that which shows the way." The Torah is that revelation of God which shows us the way we ought to live if we desire His favor and blessing.

5. MEDITATING ON GOD'S WORD

A godly man not only delights in God's ways but also meditates on them. (See Psalm 1:2.) As a result, his thoughts center on God's ways all the time. Returning to our earlier image, by virtue of his meditation on, and delight in, the Word of God, such a person is like a tree that continually draws its water from the streams that flow nearby. From the steam that flows out of God's Word, through the Holy Spirit, he is always drawing new life, new strength, and new inspiration.

I cannot overemphasize the importance of right meditation. I believe it really is the key to true prosperity. You cannot think wrong and live right. Likewise, you cannot live right and think wrong. In other words, your thinking will determine the course of your life.

Thus, this is the complete picture of the man who is like the tree planted by the streams of water—"*in whatever he does, he prospers*" (Psalm 1:3 NASB)! We will continue our coverage of the topics of prosperity and success in the next chapter.

INHERITING THE BLESSINGS

How blessed is the man who does not walk in the counsel of the wicked, nor stand in the path of sinners, nor sit in the seat of scoffers! But his delight is in the law of the LORD, and in His law he meditates day and night. And he will be like a tree firmly planted by streams of water, which yields its fruit in its season, and its leaf does not wither; and in whatever he does, he prospers. (Psalm 1:1–3 NASB)

[Jesus said,] *Abide in Me, and I in you. As the branch cannot bear fruit of itself, unless it abides in the vine, so neither can you, unless you abide in Me. I am the vine, you are the branches; he who abides in Me, and I in him, he bears much fruit; for apart from Me you can do nothing.... If you abide in Me, and My words abide in you, ask whatever you wish, and it shall be done for you. By this is My Father glorified, that you bear much fruit, and so prove to be My disciples.*

(John 15:4–5, 7–8 NASB)

22

MATERIAL PROVISION,
PART 2: TITHING

In the previous chapter, we looked at the all-inclusive promise of prosperity and success given to us in Psalm 1:1–3 and the conditions we are required to meet in order to realize those blessings. In this chapter, I want to carry that theme a little further and explore some additional promises of blessing and prosperity, especially those that have one particular scriptural condition attached to them.

ARE WE ROBBING GOD?

The first passage of Scripture we will consider is Malachi 3:7–12. Earlier, we noted that Malachi is the last prophet of the Old Testament. Approximately one thousand years earlier, the Lord, through Moses, had brought His people to the entrance of the promised land. God had placed before them a way of life. He had promised that if they would listen to His voice and obey His commandments, they would be blessed and prosper as no other nation had ever known blessing and prosperity. However, the Lord also warned them that if they did not keep His conditions and

His commandments, they would suffer the opposite results. They would incur loss, harm, defeat, and poverty. All this we saw in vivid detail in our study of Deuteronomy 28.

In the book of Malachi, God more or less sums up a thousand years of the history of Israel. Unfortunately, on the whole, it is a rather discouraging summary. God points out that, for the most part, the Israelites failed to meet His conditions. Therefore, they failed to enjoy the blessings and provision He wanted to make available to them. In the following verses from the third chapter of Malachi, the Lord points out one particular way in which they failed to meet His conditions.

> *"From the days of your fathers you have turned aside from My statutes, and have not kept them.* [This is the overview of Israel's history.] *Return to Me, and I will return to you,"* says the LORD *of hosts. "But you say, 'How shall we return?'* [That is a specific question voiced by the people of Israel, and God is very specific in His answer.] *Will a man rob God? Yet you are robbing Me! But you say, 'How have we robbed Thee?'* [God's answer is clear!] *In tithes and offerings."*
> (Malachi 3:7–8 NASB)

According to this passage, to fail to give God His due out of our finances is to rob Him! If, by chance, you are not familiar with the term *tithe*, it is an old English word for a tenth. "To tithe" means to give God the first tenth of everything we receive in income. It is important that it is the *first* tenth. We set it aside before we do anything else with the rest of our money. An offering would be anything we give to God beyond the tithe.

In specific terms, Israel had been robbing God by withholding their tithes and other contributions. What was the result? Instead of receiving a blessing, Israel received a curse. In most cases, everything we receive is either a blessing or a curse—there is not much in between.

BRING THE WHOLE TITHE

As we have established, obedience brings blessings; disobedience brings curses. This principle is reaffirmed in Malachi 3:9–10:

> "You are cursed with a curse, for you are robbing Me, the whole nation of you! [Now God gives them the remedy.] Bring the whole tithe into the storehouse, so that there may be food in My house, and test Me now in this," says the LORD of hosts, "if I will not open for you the windows of heaven, and pour out for you a blessing until it overflows."   (NASB)

God appoints a way by which He wants Israel to test Him. He explains, "If you will do what I require, then you will see what I will do." When the Lord speaks about opening "the windows of heaven," it is clear that these windows are under His sole control. There is no way for us to reach up to heaven and open its windows! That is something only God can do. And unless God does it, it will not happen.

Thus, in so many words, the Lord says, "If you will do the simple thing on earth that I require of you—if you will bring all the tithes into the storehouse—then I will do in heaven what you cannot do. I will open its windows and pour out a blessing upon you until it is overflowing."

The Lord elaborates upon this promise in the next two verses:

> "Then I will rebuke the devourer for you, so that it may not destroy the fruits of the ground; nor will your vine in the field cast its grapes," says the LORD of hosts. "And all the nations will call you blessed, for you shall be a delightful land," says the LORD of hosts.   (Malachi 3:11–12 NASB)

BLESSINGS FROM TITHES AND OFFERINGS

To briefly review, God gives an overview of Israel's history, pointing out where they have failed to meet His conditions and therefore failed to enjoy His blessings. In citing these failures, He reminds them of one of the great, basic conditions He had laid down—that they bring their tithes and offerings to Him.

Then God promises the Israelites three specific blessings if they will change their ways so that they faithfully tithe and contribute to Him. First, He says, *"I will...open for you the windows of heaven, and pour out for you a blessing"* (Malachi 3:10). As I have pointed out already, only God can open the windows of heaven.

Second, He promises, *"I will rebuke the devourer"* (verse 11). That means God will rebuke *everything* that is eating up your prosperity, your health, and your well-being; He will deal with every devouring influence and force—they will not be able to devour any longer.

Third, God states, *"All the nations will call you blessed"* (verse 12). God's people will be a testimony of His faithfulness. Those around them will take note and acknowledge this fact.

A STATE OF CONTINUAL LACK

Let's take a moment now to compare what we have read in Malachi to what God says to Israel in the first chapter of the book of Haggai. Haggai was another of God's prophets. Through the prophet, the Lord is essentially rebuking His people for the same sin of not putting Him first in their finances.

> *Now therefore, thus says the LORD of hosts, "Consider your ways! You have sown much, but harvest little; you eat, but there is not enough to be satisfied; you drink, but there is not enough to become drunk; you put on clothing, but no one is*

warm enough; and he who earns, earns wages to put into a
purse with holes."   (Haggai 1:5–6 NASB)

Have you ever felt this way? That all the money you put into
your purse or wallet somehow slips out through a hole, and you
never get the benefit of it? God points out to the Israelites that this
is essentially what is happening to them. But He also tells them
what to do about it:

> *Consider your ways! Go up to the mountains, bring wood and*
> *rebuild the temple, that I may be pleased with it and be glori-*
> *fied.*   (verse 7–8 NASB)

God is saying, "Do what I require of you, and I will deal with
the devourer who is making holes in your purses, eating away your
livelihood and your income." He further says,

> *You look for much, but behold, it comes to little; when you*
> *bring it home, I blow it away.*   (verse 9 NASB)

What the Lord describes here happens to many people, especially during days of inflation or economic recession. We look for
much, but somehow it turns to little. Although we earn money,
we just cannot make it stretch far enough to go around. God says
there is a reason: we are not putting Him first in our finances.
Accordingly, He says,

> *And I called for a drought on the land, on the mountains, on*
> *the grain, on the new wine, on the oil, on what the ground pro-*
> *duces, on men, on cattle, and on all the labor of your hands.*
>   (verse 11 NASB)

The major error the Israelites were making, both in the days
of Haggai and in the days of Malachi, was simply this: they were
failing to honor God with their finances. Israel was trying to do its
own thing—"looking after number one." By so doing, they were

neglecting the Lord. As a result, although they worked hard and seemed to be earning sufficient money, they never had enough to go around. Again, does that sound familiar? Do you meet people like that today? Are you perhaps one of those people?

God clearly states the remedy: *"Bring the whole tithe into the storehouse…, and test Me now in this"* (Malachi 3:10). He is saying, "Don't cheat on your tithe. Bring Me the whole amount. If you will bring Me the full tithe, I will see to your financial and material needs."

Tithing is simple, specific—and scriptural. Anybody can divide by ten. In any monetary system that is decimal-based, it simply means moving the decimal point one place to the left. For example, if you've earned $320.00, your tithe is $32.00. If you've earned $514.00, your tithe is $51.40. It is not difficult. I can testify to this on the basis of many years of personal experience: tithing works!

HONORING GOD WITH OUR FINANCES

The overriding principle is that we should honor God in everything, and that includes our finances and our wealth. Proverbs 3:9–10 says:

> *Honor the LORD with your wealth, with the firstfruits of all your crops; then your barns will be filled to overflowing, and your vats will brim over with new wine.* (NIV)

Please notice that we honor the Lord when we put Him first in our finances. Moreover, we need to understand that tithing was not instituted under the Law of Moses, as many people suppose. Tithing began with Abraham. It is first mentioned in the Bible in the fourteenth chapter of Genesis, where Abraham had a significant meeting with a man named Melchizedek. This is what the Bible says about that encounter:

*Then Melchizedek king of Salem brought out bread and wine.
He was priest of God Most High, and he blessed Abram
[Abraham], saying, "Blessed be Abram by God Most High,
Creator of heaven and earth. And blessed be God Most High,
who delivered your enemies into your hand."*

(Genesis 14:18–20 niv)

This is the blessing that Melchizedek, as God's priest, pronounced on God's servant Abraham. Notice how Abraham
responded to the blessing of this priest:

Then Abram gave him a tenth of everything.   (verse 20 niv)

Tithing has at least two important purposes. First, it is a way
to respond to the blessings God has given us. Second, it is a way
to honor God's priest. Abraham first practiced tithing in order to
honor God's priest Melchizedek. Because Abraham is our spiritual father—the father of all who believe (see Romans 4:11)—we
need to follow his example. We are required to walk in the steps
of his faith; and one of the primary steps of his faith was tithing.

The seventh chapter of Hebrews says that Jesus Christ is our
high priest *"according to the order of Melchizedek"* (verses 11, 17
nasb). It also emphasizes the fact that Melchizedek, as a priest,
collected a tenth from Abraham.

*But the one whose genealogy is not traced from them [the
Levitical priests] collected a tenth from Abraham, and
blessed the one who had the promises.*   (Hebrews 7:6 nasb)

We therefore honor our high priest, Jesus Christ, when we
practice tithing.

ACKNOWLEDGING THE SOURCE OF OUR SUPPLY

To conclude, tithing is our response to God's blessings, and it
is the way we honor God with our material resources. Please bear

in mind that the tithe is to be brought *"into the storehouse"* (Malachi 3:10 NASB). As I understand it, the "storehouses" are the places from which you obtain your seed—both to eat and to sow. Thus, tithing into the storehouse is the way you acknowledge the Source of your supply. I will express this concept with a little proverb: "If you eat in a Cracker Barrel restaurant, you do not pay your bill at Denny's."

If we meet the conditions God sets forth in His Word, then we can be sure He will do His part and give us overflowing blessings. Perhaps the Holy Spirit is speaking to you now through what we have covered in this chapter. Here is an opportunity to respond. By declaring the simple prayer that follows, you can let the Lord know your intention to honor Him and meet His conditions for prosperity.

> Lord, I want to obey in this matter of tithing. I want to honor You in this manner. I believe that as I bring the whole tithe into the storehouse, You will open the windows of heaven, and You will pour out a blessing upon me. Amen.

INHERITING THE BLESSINGS

> *"Bring the whole tithe into the storehouse, so that there may be food in My house, and test Me now in this," says the* LORD *of hosts, "if I will not open for you the windows of heaven, and pour out for you a blessing until it overflows. Then I will rebuke the devourer for you, so that it may not destroy the fruits of the ground; nor will your vine in the field cast its grapes," says the* LORD *of hosts. "And all the nations will call you blessed, for you shall be a delightful land," says the* LORD *of hosts.* (Malachi 3:10–12 NASB)

> *Honor the* LORD *with your wealth, with the firstfruits of all your crops; then your barns will be filled to overflowing, and your vats will brim over with new wine.*
> (Proverbs 3:9–10 NIV)

23

MATERIAL PROVISION, PART 3: SOWING AND REAPING

In the two previous chapters, we have focused on prosperity—an important aspect of our inheritance in the land of God's promises. In our survey of Psalm 1, we saw that stability and success are promised to those who choose good counsel and wise friendships, and who delight in and meditate on God's law. We also saw that the scriptural principle of tithing is a condition of blessing—and a primary test of our willingness to trust and obey God. In this chapter, we will cover another scriptural principle upon which God's promise to prosper us is based. If we understand this principle, it will take us even further into this area of prosperity.

GIVING "HILARIOUSLY"

The eighth and ninth chapters of 2 Corinthians deal with the theme of giving money to God. The background of these chapters is that the apostle Paul was writing to request an offering from various churches for certain believers who were in financial need. One of the churches to whom Paul was corresponding was the fellowship at Corinth, which had promised to provide a contribution. In his letter, Paul explains how he wants the administration of the gift to be arranged. In doing so, he outlines some of the important motives and principles that should govern our giving to God. Thus, Paul's instructions are very important for you and me, as well, because the same motives and principles are valid for us today. Let's begin our overview of these principles by looking at a passage from 2 Corinthians 9:

> So I thought it necessary to urge the brothers to visit you in advance and finish the arrangements for the generous gift you had promised. Then it will be ready as a generous gift, not as one grudgingly given. [Paul is emphasizing that motives are very important.] Remember this: Whoever sows sparingly will also reap sparingly, and whoever sows generously will also reap generously.   (2 Corinthians 9:5–6 NIV)

When Paul uses the words *sow* and *reap*, he is employing the terminology of agriculture but applying it to money. "Sowing" is giving money, and "reaping" is receiving money. Please bear these concepts in mind as we continue, because they are significant. Paul then gives another principle relating to motive:

> Each man should give what he has decided in his heart to give, not reluctantly or under compulsion, for God loves a cheerful giver.   (2 Corinthians 9:7 NIV)

The Greek phrase translated "*a cheerful giver*" means "a hilarious giver." I wonder how many of us are "hilarious" in our giving? I have seen people in very poor, backward, and underprivileged nations of the Third World giving hilariously to God, far above their tithe. And I have seen how God has blessed them.

GRACE THAT ABOUNDS

Let us continue by reading the next verse, 2 Corinthians 9:8, which we previously looked at in chapter 5 of this book, although in a different Bible translation:

And God is able to make all grace abound to you, so that in all things at all times, having all that you need, you will abound in every good work.   (NIV)

What a rich verse! There are two *abound's* and five *all's* (the fifth in the form of "every"). Taken in its totality, this promise leaves no room for lack or insufficiency in the application of God's grace to any area of our lives.

The key word in these Scriptures on giving is *"grace."* Did you know that giving is a grace? It is one of the Christian graces that spring from the grace of God.

INCREASE THROUGH SCATTERING

Paul maintains this train of thought in the next verse when he quotes Psalm 112:9:

As it is written: "He [the righteous man] has scattered abroad his gifts to the poor; his righteousness endures forever."   (1 Corinthians 9:9 NIV)

Please notice that there is a very close connection between giving to the poor and having a righteousness that endures. The word *"scattered"* is another agricultural reference, suggesting a person sowing seed in his or her field. We can apply this reference to Jesus's sacrifice for us. When Jesus died on the cross, He sowed the seed of His own body on behalf of us who were spiritually poverty-stricken. In 2 Corinthians 8, Paul wrote about the divine exchange that took place by God's foreordained purpose and through His grace at the cross. Jesus bore the poverty curse that had come upon the human race through its disobedience in order that we, in turn, might be partakers of His wealth.

For you know the grace of our Lord Jesus Christ, that though He was rich, yet for your sakes He became poor, so that you through His poverty might become rich.

(2 Corinthians 8:9 NIV)

When Jesus hung on the cross, He was under the curse of poverty. He was *"in the lack of all things"* (Deuteronomy 28:48 NASB). The cross is the basis of the great exchange. The foundation of all God's provision is this: Jesus took the poverty curse so we might receive His abundance through faith. That is *grace!* And that grace is manifested in our lives by the fact that God makes it *"abound to* [us], *so that in all things at all times, having all that* [we] *need,* [we] *will abound in every good work"* (2 Corinthians 9:8 NIV).

Thus, the spiritual principle Paul brings out from the agricultural principle of sowing and reaping is that *increase comes through scattering.* In other words, the measure in which we scatter, or sow, will determine the measure in which we reap. One of the divine paradoxes of nature is that *scattering leads to increase, but withholding leads to poverty.* Imagine a farmer who is delighted because he has in his possession some tremendously wonderful seed, but who says to himself, "This seed is so good that I'm just going to hold on to it. I'm not going to sow any of it in the ground." How much return will that farmer reap from that seed? Nothing!

Throughout the Bible, we see that stinginess ultimately leads to poverty. Therefore, if we want increase, we must scatter and spread our seed.

A MARK OF RIGHTEOUSNESS

Let's turn now to Psalm 112, the psalm Paul quoted from in 2 Corinthians 9:9. We will especially consider verses that depict a man of outstanding righteousness, whose life is built firmly on the foundation of God's Word and the fear of the Lord.

Praise the LORD. Blessed is the man who fears the LORD, who finds great delight in His commands. His children will be mighty in the land; the generation of the upright will be blessed. [That is the promise of continuing blessing from generation to generation we looked at in an earlier chapter of this book.] *Wealth and riches are in his house, and his righteousness endures forever....* [Notice the direct connection between righteousness, wealth, and riches in his house.] *Good will come to him who is generous and lends freely....* [That is the same principle again: increase comes through scattering.] *His heart is secure, he will have no fear; in the end he will look in triumph on his foes. He has scattered abroad his gifts to the poor, his righteousness endures forever; his horn will be lifted high in honor.*

(Psalm 112:1–3, 5, 8–9 NIV)

We see again that scattering—giving generously and not withholding—is a mark of righteousness. It establishes our righteousness, and it ensures that we will reap. We can conclude, therefore, that lending and giving generously are connected with righteousness, security, and prosperity. These go together in God's purposes, and they can never be separated.

The paradox of scattering and withholding—*that scattering leads to increase, but withholding leads to poverty*—is also expressed in Proverbs 11:24:

One man gives freely, yet gains even more; another withholds unduly, but comes to poverty. (NIV)

Withholding from God and from the poor what we should be giving to them will bring us poverty. However, as we have seen from the other passages we have been looking at in this chapter, if we are giving freely by scattering in faith, according to the principles of God's Word, we are giving to God and to those who are in need—which, in turn, will cause us to gain even more. Please bear in mind that all giving must be done in faith, because *"without faith it is impossible to please God"* (Hebrews 11:6 NIV). That is the reason we give before we receive, and scatter before we reap; it is always the faith principle at work.

INVESTING WISELY

We have seen how Paul applies the basic principles of agriculture to the handling of money in God's kingdom, and this brings us to some very practical applications of God's truth. If a farmer desires to get the best crops from his land, he needs to observe three simple principles:

1. He needs to choose good soil.

2. He needs to make proper preparation of the soil.

3. He needs to manage his whole enterprise well.

For example, if a farmer were to walk down the main street of his city scattering his seed right and left into the gutters, he would never reap a thing. *Where* we scatter makes a great deal of difference. That is why, in the hope of a good harvest, the farmer invests in good soil, good preparation, and good management.

I believe the same principles are true with regard to our investment in God's kingdom. If we sow wisely, we will reap abundantly. Accordingly, we should never give on impulse, out of an emotional urge. Rather, we should first sincerely and carefully seek out those ministries and enterprises of God that are based on proper scriptural principles. We should invest in those that are working in good soil, where there is proper preparation to ensure their maximum return, and where the management is good, ethical, and honest.

I fear that many of God's people miss out on the blessings of sowing because they do not understand that you must sow before you reap, and that you must scatter in order to increase. In addition, some of those who *do* practice sowing miss out on the blessings because they sow where there is not going to be a good return. They invest in unworthy enterprises or unscriptural operations that are poorly managed. As a result, they do not get the return they were hoping for.

COMMIT YOUR FINANCES TO GOD

As you consider your own patterns and practices of giving to promote God's purposes, let me suggest that you ask yourself these three questions:

1. Am I flowing with God's purposes in my life?
2. Am I following the basic godly principles outlined in this chapter?
3. Are my motives right?

If the answer to these questions is yes, I believe the end result for you will be God's blessings of prosperity and abundance.

Would you like to take a moment to commit to the Lord this whole matter of giving? If you wish to dedicate this important area of your life to the Lord, you can do so now with this simple, brief prayer:

Lord, I recognize You as the wellspring of all my resources. I want to honor You in the way I handle my finances—and I want to place myself in a position to receive the promise of blessing from You in this area.

I want to sow wisely, so I can reap well. I commit this area of my life—and all of my resources—to You now. In Jesus's name, amen.

INHERITING THE BLESSINGS

Remember this: Whoever sows sparingly will also reap sparingly, and whoever sows generously will also reap generously. Each man should give what he has decided in his heart to give, not reluctantly or under compulsion, for God loves a cheerful giver. And God is able to make all grace abound to you, so that in all things at all times, having all that you need, you will abound in every good work. (2 Corinthians 9:6–8 NIV)

For you know the grace of our Lord Jesus Christ, that though he was rich, yet for your sakes he became poor, so that you through his poverty might become rich.

(2 Corinthians 8:9 NIV)

24

HEALING, PART 1: RESTORATION THROUGH GOD'S WORD

Our journey through the land of God's promises now brings us to another major area of our inheritance: *healing and health.* As we have seen with all of God's marvelous promises we have explored throughout this book, it is God's own Word that is the great, basic foundation for the healing and health He has provided for His people.

"I AM YOUR HEALER"

One of the first specific revelations of Himself that God gave the Israelites after He redeemed them out of slavery in Egypt, and they became His covenant people, was that He was their Healer. In Exodus 15:26, the Lord said to Israel,

If you will give earnest heed to the voice of the LORD your God, and do what is right in His sight, and give ear to His commandments, and keep all His statutes, I will put none of the diseases on you which I have put on the Egyptians; for I, the LORD, am your healer. (NASB)

Precisely the same word translated *"your healer"* (*rapha*) is the word in modern Hebrew for "your doctor." The word has not changed its meaning in over three thousand years of the history of the Hebrew language. The Lord says emphatically to the Israelites, "I am your Doctor." He unites *rapha* with His own name, *Jehovah*, "the Lord," and He makes a covenant with them to confirm it.

God's name and covenant never change. In other words, the Lord's position and function as the Healer of His people are united with His name and His covenant; therefore, *they are unchanging.*

Many centuries after God revealed Himself to the Israelites as their Healer, Jesus came to Israel as Savior and Redeemer, fulfilling the promises of the Messiah. Matthew 8:16–17 is a passage we began to look at in chapter 4, "Physical Benefits of Redemption." Let us read it again:

> *And when evening had come, they brought to Him* [Jesus] *many who were demon-possessed; and He cast out the spirits with a word, and healed all who were ill in order that what was spoken through Isaiah the prophet might be fulfilled, saying, "He Himself took our infirmities, and carried away our diseases."* (NASB)

Jesus *"healed all who were ill,"* in fulfillment of Isaiah's prophecy. As the Messiah, He manifested the unchanging nature of God as the Healer of His people. In John 14:9–10, Jesus says,

> *He who has seen Me has seen the Father.… The words that I say to you I do not speak on My own initiative, but the Father abiding in Me does His works.* (NASB)

In saying this, Jesus indicates that His healing ministry did not initiate or proceed from Himself—it was the expression of the healing nature of God the Father and His healing covenant with His people.

SAVED, HEALED, AND DELIVERED

As emphasized above, the foundation of God's provision of healing and health for His people is His Word, the Scriptures. Psalm 107 depicts the affliction of some who rebelled against God's commandments:

> *Fools, because of their rebellious way, and because of their iniquities, were afflicted. Their soul abhorred all kinds of food; and they drew near to the gates of death.*
>
> (Psalm 107:17–18 NASB)

In a dramatic way, the psalmist is saying that these "*fools*" had exhausted all medical help. There was no further hope for them, and they were at the very "*gates of death*"—simply waiting to die. But in the verses that follow, we read that they cried out to the Lord. My comment on that development is that people often wait very late to pray for healing. These people were right at death's door—and finally it occurred to them to pray! How many times are we like that in our circumstances? We often do not pray until there is absolutely no other source of help but God.

> *Then they cried out to the LORD in their trouble; He saved them out of their distresses. He sent His word and healed them, and delivered them from their destructions.*
>
> (Psalm 107:19–20 NASB)

In the above passage, we find three successive statements about how God intervened when the people at the gates of death cried out to Him: He *saved* them, He *healed* them, and He *delivered* them. I believe those responses represent the three great ways in which God intervenes in mercy to help us in our lives. He saves, He heals, and He delivers. Each of those actions meets a specific area of need. He saves us from sin. He heals us from sickness. And He delivers us from the power of Satan.

Basically, His provision for each of these three acts of mercy—
to meet these three areas of our need—is in His Word. *"He sent
His word and healed them"* (Psalm 107:20 NASB). It was *through His
Word* that He answered their prayer—their cry for help when they
were at death's door.

It is essential for us to understand that God's answer to our
need is primarily in His Word. If we ignore His Word, then we
really do not have any right to expect Him to meet our needs. But
if we will turn to His Word, and seek Him through the Word, we
will find that, in His Word, He does meet all our needs—spiritual
and physical.

GOD'S WORD IS OUR MEDICINE

Let's look next at Proverbs 4:20–22, a passage of Scripture
in which God offers us total healing and health. This particular
promise is very precious to me. I was once confined to the hospital
for an entire year, having a condition that doctors apparently were
not able to heal. But when I sought God through His Word, He
granted me that which He had promised—healing and health. It
was not a temporary healing; it was a full and complete restoration
of health that has remained.

This Scripture opens with the words *"My son."* Through this
passage, God is instructing you and me as His children. Jesus has
said that healing is *"the children's bread"* (Matthew 15:26 NASB,
NIV, NKJV, KJV). The Father has provided the promise of healing
for all His children. Please read carefully these beautiful truths:

> *My son, give attention to my words; incline your ear to my
> sayings. Do not let them depart from your sight; keep them
> in the midst of your heart. For they are life to those who find
> them, and health to all their whole body.*
>
> (Proverbs 4:20–22 NASB)

When I lay sick in that hospital bed, I reached out by faith and grasped hold of the last phrase of the above passage: *"health to all their whole body."* I said to myself, "If God is offering me health in all of my body, then there can be no room for sickness. Wherever there is health, there is no sickness. If I can have health in all of my body, that means I can be perfectly well and not sick."

Then I looked again at this passage and saw that God also said, *"They are life to those who find them, and health to all their whole body."* I wondered, "What is denoted by the word 'they'?" When I reread the previous verses, I saw that *"they"* refers to godly words and sayings: *"My son, give attention to my words; incline your ear to my sayings."* I realized that if I could find God-given words and sayings, they would be life to me—and health to my whole body.

At that time, I had a Bible with marginal notes showing alternative translations of various words in the text. The alternative reading for *"health"* was *"medicine."* That pleased me even more! I said to myself, "If I'm well, God's words and sayings will keep me well; and if I'm sick, they will be my medicine."

Right then, I decided, in a very simple, childlike way, to take God's Word as my medicine. It so happened that I was a hospital attendant myself, and I had often given people their medicine. I asked myself, "Now, how do people take their medicine?"

The answer was, "Usually, three times daily, after meals."

So I decided, "I'm going to take God's Word in the same way. Three times daily, after meals, I'm going to take it as my medicine."

"TAKE AS DIRECTED"

Then the Lord spoke very clearly to my mind, saying, "When the doctor gives a patient medicine in a bottle, the directions for taking it are on the bottle. The directions for taking this medicine of Mine are on the bottle. You'd better read them."

So I looked again at Proverbs 4:20–22 (NASB), and I saw that there were four clear directions for taking God's Word as medicine.

1. *"Give attention"* (verse 20). We must listen very closely to what God is saying.

2. *"Incline your ear"* (verse 20). I understood this to mean that I should bow my head. In other words, I was to be humble and teachable. I believe it indicates we are never to argue with God, never to think that we know everything, but instead be willing to let God teach us. So many people read the Bible with their minds already made up as to what God "ought" to be saying. As a result, if He says something different, they cannot hear it—because they have not inclined their ear.

3. *"Do not let them depart from your sight"* (verse 21). We must keep our eyes focused on the promises of God, and never let them waver.

4. *"Keep them in the midst of your heart"* (verse 21). We must let God's Word settle right down into the very central area of our being: our heart, mind, and spirit—that part of us out of which all of our life ultimately originates. When God's Word gets in there, it will bring us healing and health.

Over time, through that very simple means of taking God's Word as my medicine, three times daily, after meals, in a climate that was extremely bad for my condition, with everything in the natural against me—I received exactly what God had promised me: *"health to all their* [my] *whole body"* (verse 22).

How about you? Are you seeking the promise of God for healing and health in your life? Based on my own experience, I can assure you that if you are in need, and you will take God's Word as your medicine in the same way, it will do the same for you.

Give God's Word your attention. Incline your ear to it. Focus your eyes on it. Keep it in the midst of your heart. If you do, it will

be life to you and health to your whole body—a wonderful fulfillment of God's promise to you of healing and health.

INHERITING THE BLESSINGS

*And when evening had come, they brought to Him [Jesus]
many who were demon-possessed; and He cast out the spirits
with a word, and healed all who were ill in order that what
was spoken through Isaiah the prophet might be fulfilled,
saying, "He Himself took our infirmities, and carried away
our diseases."*   (Matthew 8:16–17 NASB)

*My son, give attention to my words; incline your ear to my
sayings. Do not let them depart from your sight; keep them
in the midst of your heart. For they are life to those who find
them, and health to all their whole body.*

                        (Proverbs 4:20–22 NASB)

25

HEALING, PART 2: RESTORATION THROUGH PRAYER

Over the course of this book, we have learned how to progressively enter into God's provision for us as His people. As we identify our needs, locate the corresponding promises, and meet the conditions, we can claim the provisions in God's Word that apply to each area of our lives. Let me emphasize once more that God's provision is in His promises, and the promises are our wonderful inheritance in Christ.

We are currently focusing on the area of healing and health. In addition to God's provision found in His Word, there is another way in which He makes healing and health available to us. This promise is not as familiar to many Christians as it should be, and yet it is very important. It is clearly stated in the fifth chapter of the book of James:

> *Is any one of you in trouble? He should pray. Is anyone happy? Let him sing songs of praise. Is any one of you sick? He should call the elders of the church to pray over him and anoint him with oil in the name of the Lord.* (James 5:13–14 NIV)

In this passage, James envisions three different situations in which we may find ourselves, and recommends how we should respond in each of those situations. If we are in trouble, the answer is to pray. If we are happy, our response is to sing songs of praise. But what if we are sick? Many of us might say we should call the doctor. However, that is not what James says. He tells us to *"call the elders of the church."* I wonder how many thousands there are among the people of God who, when they get sick, are not even aware of this direction in the Scriptures.

First, I want to be very clear in saying that I strongly believe in the service that doctors provide to humanity. There is absolutely nothing wrong with visiting the doctor or going to the hospital when you are sick. I thank God for the ministry of doctors, nurses, and all others in the health care profession who are genuinely attending to the needs of sick humanity.

Thus, it is not wrong to call for the doctor. But it *is wrong* not to also call for the elders of the church. *"Is any one of you sick? He should call the elders of the church to pray over him and anoint him with oil in the name of the Lord."*

Some people might say, "Well, perhaps that advice is out-of-date." But such a response is actually inconsistent with the rest of the passage, because two other directives are given in it: if we are in trouble, we are to pray; if we are happy, we are to sing songs of praise. Is it out-of-date to pray? Is it out-of-date to sing songs of praise? If the answer to the first two is no, then why should it be out-of-date to call for the elders of the church to pray for you?

AN UNLIMITED PROMISE

When the elders of the church are called, they are to come and anoint the sick person with oil in the name of the Lord. Here is the promise that follows that action:

And the prayer offered in faith will make the sick person well;
the Lord will raise him up. If he has sinned, he will be forgiven.
Therefore confess your sins to each other and pray for each
other so that you may be healed. The prayer of a righteous
man is powerful and effective.   (James 5:15–16 NIV)

Where it says *"the prayer offered in faith will make the sick*
person well," the literal words from the Greek are "the prayer
of faith will *save* the sick." It is important to understand that
the Greek word for "save," *sozo*, is used in the New Testament
for *all* the provisions of God's blessing that come to us through
faith in Jesus Christ. It is used for the deliverance of our souls
from sin, the deliverance of our bodies from sickness, and
many other provisions of God's mercy. Thus, *salvation* is an
all-inclusive word that encompasses healing for those who are
ill. Of course, the phrase *"will make the sick person well"* is a
legitimate translation. But it is important to see that it is just
one of the different ways we may translate the original word
meaning "to save."

The promise in the above passage from James is that prayer,
offered on the right basis and in faith, will bring healing to any
believer who needs it. There is no limitation as to how many believers or what kind of believers may be healed. The question is simply,
"Is any one of you sick?" (James 5:14 NIV). Nothing more than that
is stated. There are no qualifications as to whether the sickness is
severe or slight, or whether it has been long-term or short-term. If
we meet the conditions, God will raise up the sick person. That is
the explicit promise.

CONDITIONS TO CONSIDER

Just as there have been with other promises we have looked at,
there are a number of conditions related to this promise which we
need to consider rather carefully.

CALL FOR THE ELDERS

First of all, the sick person is obligated to call for the elders of the church. The elders are obligated to pray over and anoint that person with oil in the name of the Lord. Furthermore, the elders are obligated to pray the prayer of faith.

Behind these conditions we see other implications. For instance, it is assumed that the sick believer will be a member of an assembly or a church that has recognized elders. Many people have not fulfilled that condition. However, throughout the New Testament, it is assumed that under normal circumstances, every believer will be associated with a church, fellowship, or assembly that has elders who are capable of fulfilling this function. It is also implied that the elders will be familiar with their scriptural responsibility and capable of praying in faith.

BE ANOINTED WITH OIL

What is the significance of being anointed with oil? First, it is an established practice for God's people that goes back many centuries. It was not something new in the time of the early church. It was carried over from the Old Testament to the New as part of the inheritance of God's people.

Why oil? In the original Greek, the word translated *"oil"* in the passage from James was used for "olive oil," and olive oil is a type or picture of the Holy Spirit. The clear implication is that by anointing with oil, the elders are claiming God's promise that the Holy Spirit will minister life and health to the body of the sick believer. This is in accordance with what Paul says in Romans 8:11:

> But if the Spirit of Him who raised Jesus from the dead dwells
> in you, He who raised Christ Jesus from the dead will also
> give life to your mortal bodies through His Spirit who indwells
> you.   (NASB)

One of the great ministries of the Holy Spirit is to give life to the mortal bodies of God's people. To anoint with oil is an act of obedience and faith by which the power of the Holy Spirit is released into a believer to minister life to the body, drive out illness, and replace sickness with health.

CONFESS YOUR SINS

James also tells us that if believers who are sick have unconfessed sins, they are required to confess those sins, presumably to the elders who are going to pray for them. Why do they have to confess their sins? The answer is that unconfessed sin can be a barrier to answered prayer and a hindrance to the working of God's mercy in the life of a believer. This is what the psalmist says in Psalm 66:18–19:

> *If I had cherished sin in my heart, the Lord would not have listened; but God has surely listened and heard my voice in prayer.* (NIV)

In order for our voice to be heard in prayer, we must be careful not to cherish sin in our heart. If there is something in our heart and life that should not be there, before we ask for prayer for healing, we should confess it to those who are going to pray for us. As they stand with us in faith that God has forgiven us, we know that God will listen to and hear our voice in prayer, just as the psalmist said.

We can also rest on this promise from 1 John 3:21–22:

> *Beloved, if our heart does not condemn us, we have confidence before God; and whatever we ask we receive from Him, because we keep His commandments and do the things that are pleasing in His sight.* (NASB)

If we have a sense of condemnation in our heart, it takes away our confidence that God will answer our prayers. Therefore, if there is any question of sin in our heart, we need to confess that sin and be assured of God's forgiveness before we go through the procedure for claiming healing through anointing with oil in the name of the Lord.

PRAYING IN FAITH

How can the elders fulfill their part by praying the prayer of faith? I suggest there is a threefold basis for their faith. First, they must act in obedience to the Word of God by doing what God requires. Obedience always opens the way for the blessing of God to flow. As long as we are disobedient, it is hard for us to pray in faith.

Second, the elders need to recognize the provision God has already made through the death of Jesus. For instance, Peter tells us,

> He Himself [Jesus] bore our sins in His body on the cross, that we might die to sin and live to righteousness; for by His wounds you were healed. (1 Peter 2:24 NASB)

In a certain sense, healing has already been provided through the substitutionary death of Jesus on the cross. We are not asking God to do something new or strange. We are simply laying claim to that which God has already provided through the atonement of Jesus.

Third, by anointing with oil, the elders are trusting the Holy Spirit to do what only He can do. It is not the elders who are doing the healing. God is the Healer, and He has always been the Healer of His people. He heals when we do what He requires of us.

We may put it this way: we do the possible, and God does the impossible; we do the simple, and God does the difficult. The simple is to anoint with oil and pray. When we do that in humble faith, then God does the difficult. Always remember: *we do the possible—God does the impossible.*

INHERITING THE BLESSINGS

Is any one of you sick? He should call the elders of the church to pray over him and anoint him with oil in the name of the Lord. And the prayer offered in faith will make the sick person well; the Lord will raise him up. If he has sinned, he will be forgiven. Therefore confess your sins to each other and pray for each other so that you may be healed. The prayer of a righteous man is powerful and effective.   (James 5:14–16 NIV)

But if the Spirit of Him who raised Jesus from the dead dwells in you, He who raised Christ Jesus from the dead will also give life to your mortal bodies through His Spirit who indwells you.   (Romans 8:11 NASB)

26

CONTINUING YOUR JOURNEY

It has been my goal throughout *Receiving God's Promises* to help you discover and begin claiming your inheritance as a Christian— as an heir of the kingdom of God. In so doing, I have endeavored to introduce you to your inheritance by taking you on a brief walk through the land of God's promises.

Please realize, however, that in the limited space of this book, I have been able to introduce you to only a small portion of your inheritance. The Scripture is the land of our inheritance in the form of all the promises it contains—if you will diligently take the time to seek them out and put forth the effort to apply them to your life.

May God bless you, and may the Holy Spirit guide you, as you continue your journey. In closing, I leave you with God's command to Abraham:

*Arise, walk about the land through its length and breadth; **for I will give it to you.*** (Genesis 13:17 NASB)

BIBLE PROMISES BY TOPIC

INTRODUCTION

In *Receiving God's Promises*, Derek Prince explains that "God's provision is in His promises, and the promises are our wonderful inheritance in Christ." He also reminds us that we must meet the conditions God has set forth for these promises to be fulfilled. The following are topical Bible promises related to themes Derek covers throughout this book. Some of the verses apply to more than one category even though they come under one topical area. And, as Derek says, there are many additional promises in the Bible that we are to search for as we read and study the Bible so we may faithfully apply them to our lives.

Unless otherwise indicated, all the verses in this section are taken from the *King James Easy Read Bible*. May these Scriptures encourage and establish you as you take possession of the land of your inheritance in Christ!

—*The International Publishing Team of Derek Prince Ministries*

GOD'S FAITHFULNESS TO HIS PROMISES

God is not a man, that He should lie; neither the son of man, that He should repent: has He said, and shall He not do it? or has He spoken, and shall He not make it good?

(Numbers 23:19)

Know therefore that the LORD your God, He is God the faithful God, which keeps covenant and mercy with them that love Him and keep His commandments to a thousand generations. (Deuteronomy 7:9)

Not one of all the LORD's good promises to the house of Israel failed; every one was fulfilled. (Joshua 21:45 NIV)

For verily I say to you, Till heaven and earth pass, one jot or one tittle shall in no wise pass from the law, till all be fulfilled. (Matthew 5:18)

For all the promises of God in Him are yea, and in Him Amen, to the glory of God by us. (2 Corinthians 1:20)

Let us hold fast the profession of our faith without wavering; (for He is faithful that promised). (Hebrews 10:23)

Jesus Christ the same yesterday, and to day, and for ever.

(Hebrews 13:8)

OUR OBEDIENT RESPONSE TO GOD'S PROMISES

All the paths of the LORD are mercy and truth to such as keep His covenant and His testimonies. (Psalm 25:10)

Because he has set his love upon Me, therefore will I deliver him: I will set him on high, because he has known My name. He shall call upon Me, and I will answer him: I will be with him in trouble; I will deliver him, and honor him. With long life will I satisfy him, and show him My salvation.
(Psalm 91:14–16)

My eyes stay open through the watches of the night, that I may meditate on your promises.   (Psalm 119:148 NIV)

For I spoke not to your fathers, nor commanded them in the day that I brought them out of the land of Egypt, concerning burned offerings or sacrifices: but this thing commanded I them, saying, Obey My voice, and I will be your God, and you shall be My people: and walk you in all the ways that I have commanded you, that it may be well to you.
(Jeremiah 7:22–23)

Blessed are they that hear the word of God, and keep it.
(Luke 11:28)

He that has My commandments, and keeps them, he it is that loves Me: and he that loves Me shall be loved of My Father, and I will love him, and will manifest Myself to him.
(John 14:21)

You are My friends, if you do whatsoever I command you.
(John 15:14)

According as His divine power has given to us all things that pertain to life and godliness, through the knowledge of Him that has called us to glory and virtue: whereby are given to us exceeding great and precious promises: that by these you might be partakers of the divine nature, having escaped the corruption that is in the world through lust. (2 Peter 1:3–4)

SALVATION

But as many as received Him, to them gave He power to become the sons of God, even to them that believe on His name: which were born, not of blood, nor of the will of the flesh, nor of the will of man, but of God.   (John 1:12–13)

For God so loved the world, that He gave His only begotten Son, that whosoever believes in Him should not perish, but have everlasting life. For God sent not His Son into the world to condemn the world; but that the world through Him might be saved.   (John 3:16–17)

The word is near you, even in your mouth, and in your heart: that is, the word of faith, which we preach; that if you shall confess with your mouth the Lord Jesus, and shall believe in your heart that God has raised Him from the dead, you shall be saved. For with the heart man believes to righteousness; and with the mouth confession is made to salvation.... For whosoever shall call upon the name of the Lord shall be saved.   (Romans 10:8–10, 13)

For by grace are you saved through faith; and that not of yourselves: it is the gift of God: not of works, lest any man should boast.   (Ephesians 2:8–9)

The Lord is not slack concerning His promise, as some men count slackness; but is long-suffering to us-ward, not willing that any should perish, but that all should come to repentance.   (2 Peter 3:9)

Behold, I stand at the door, and knock: if any man hear My voice, and open the door, I will come in to him, and will sup [dine] with him, and he with Me.   (Revelation 3:20)

FORGIVENESS

Blessed is he whose transgression is forgiven, whose sin is covered. Blessed is the man to whom the LORD *imputes not iniquity, and in whose spirit there is no guile.* (Psalm 32:1–2)

As far as the east is from the west, so far has He removed our transgressions from us. (Psalm 103:12)

He that covers his sins shall not prosper: but whoso confesses and forsakes them shall have mercy. (Proverbs 28:13)

I, even I, am He that blots out your transgressions for My own sake, and will not remember your sins. (Isaiah 43:25)

For if you forgive men their trespasses, your heavenly Father will also forgive you: but if you forgive not men their trespasses, neither will your Father forgive your trespasses.
(Matthew 6:14–15)

To Him give all the prophets witness, that through His name whosoever believes in Him shall receive remission of sins.
(Acts 10:43)

In whom we have redemption through His blood, the forgiveness of sins, according to the riches of His grace.
(Ephesians 1:7)

If we confess our sins, He is faithful and just to forgive us our sins, and to cleanse us from all unrighteousness.
(1 John 1:9)

My little children, these things write I to you, that you sin not. And if any man sin, we have an advocate with the Father, Jesus Christ the righteous: and He is the propitiation for our sins: and not for ours only, but also for the sins of the whole world. (1 John 2:1–2)

GIFT OF THE HOLY SPIRIT

I indeed baptize you with water to repentance: but He that comes after me is mightier than I, whose shoes I am not worthy to bear: He shall baptize you with the Holy Ghost [Spirit], and with fire. (Matthew 3:11)

If you then, being evil, know how to give good gifts to your children: how much more shall your heavenly Father give the Holy Spirit to them that ask Him? (Luke 11:13)

If you love Me, keep My commandments. And I will pray the Father, and He shall give you another Comforter, that He may abide with you for ever; even the Spirit of truth; whom the world cannot receive, because it sees Him not, neither knows Him: but you know Him; for He dwells with you, and shall be in you. I will not leave you comfortless: I will come to you.... The Comforter, which is the Holy Ghost, whom the Father will send in My name, He shall teach you all things, and bring all things to your remembrance, whatsoever I have said to you. (John 14:15–18, 26)

However when He, the Spirit of truth, is come, He will guide you into all truth: for He shall not speak of Himself; but whatsoever He shall hear, that shall He speak: and He will show you things to come. He shall glorify Me: for He shall receive of Mine, and shall show it to you. All things that the Father has

*are Mine: therefore said I, that He shall take of Mine, and
shall show it to you.*   (John 16:13–15)

*But you shall receive power, after that the Holy Ghost [Spirit]
is come upon you: and you shall be witnesses to Me both in
Jerusalem, and in all Judaea, and in Samaria, and to the
uttermost part of the earth.*   (Acts 1:8)

*Then Peter said to them, Repent, and be baptized every one of
you in the name of Jesus Christ for the remission of sins, and
you shall receive the gift of the Holy Ghost [Spirit]. For the
promise is to you, and to your children, and to all that are afar
off, even as many as the Lord our God shall call.*
                    (Acts 2:38–39)

*But as it is written, Eye has not seen, nor ear heard, neither
have entered into the heart of man, the things which God has
prepared for them that love Him. But God has revealed them
to us by His Spirit: for the Spirit searches all things, yea, the
deep things of God.… Now we have received, not the spirit of
the world, but the spirit which is of God; that we might know
the things that are freely given to us of God.*
                    (1 Corinthians 2:9–10, 12)

*And because you are sons, God has sent forth the Spirit of His
Son into your hearts, crying, Abba, Father.*   (Galatians 4:6)

NEWNESS OF LIFE/SANCTIFICATION

*A new heart also will I give you, and a new Spirit will I put
within you: and I will take away the stony heart out of your
flesh, and I will give you a heart of flesh. And I will put My
Spirit within you, and cause you to walk in My statutes, and*

you shall keep My judgments, and do them.

(Ezekiel 36:26–27)

Therefore we are buried with Him by baptism into death: that like as Christ was raised up from the dead by the glory of the Father, even so we also should walk in newness of life.

(Romans 6:4)

Therefore if any man be in Christ, he is a new creature: old things are passed away; behold, all things are become new.

(2 Corinthians 5:17)

I am crucified with Christ: nevertheless I live; yet not I, but Christ lives in me: and the life which I now live in the flesh I live by the faith of the Son of God, who loved me, and gave Himself for me. (Galatians 2:20)

Christ also loved the church, and gave Himself for it; that He might sanctify and cleanse it with the washing of water by the word, that He might present it to Himself a glorious church, not having spot, or wrinkle, or any such thing; but that it should be holy and without blemish. (Ephesians 5:25–27)

And the very God of peace sanctify you wholly; and I pray God your whole spirit and soul and body be preserved blameless to the coming of our Lord Jesus Christ. Faithful is He that calls you, who also will do it. (1 Thessalonians 5:23–24)

Let us be glad and rejoice, and give honor to Him: for the marriage of the Lamb is come, and His wife has made herself ready. And to her was granted that she should be arrayed in fine linen, clean and white: for the fine linen is the righteousness of saints. (Revelation 19:7–8)

INHERITANCE FROM GOD THROUGH CHRIST

Moses My servant is dead; now therefore arise, go over this Jordan, you, and all this people, to the land which I do give to them, even to the children of Israel. Every place that the sole of your foot shall tread upon, that have I given to you, as I said to Moses.   (Joshua 1:2–3)

For you know the grace of our Lord Jesus Christ, that, though He was rich, yet for your sakes He became poor, that you through His poverty might be rich.   (2 Corinthians 8:9)

Christ has redeemed us from the curse of the law, being made a curse for us: for it is written, Cursed is every one that hangs on a tree: that the blessing of Abraham might come on the Gentiles through Jesus Christ; that we might receive the promise of the Spirit through faith.   (Galatians 3:13–14)

In whom [Jesus Christ] you also trusted, after that you heard the word of truth, the gospel of your salvation: in whom also after that you believed, you were sealed with that holy Spirit of promise, which is the earnest of our inheritance until the redemption of the purchased possession, to the praise of His glory.   (Ephesians 1:13–14)

Giving thanks to the Father, which has made us meet to be partakers of the inheritance of the saints in light: who has delivered us from the power of darkness, and has translated us into the kingdom of His dear Son: in whom we have redemption through His blood, even the forgiveness of sins.
                                    (Colossians 1:12–14)

And for this cause He is the mediator of the new testament, that by means of death, for the redemption of the

transgressions that were under the first testament, they which are called might receive the promise of eternal inheritance.
(Hebrews 9:15)

Blessed be the God and Father of our Lord Jesus Christ, which according to His abundant mercy has begotten us again to a lively [living] hope by the resurrection of Jesus Christ from the dead, to an inheritance incorruptible, and undefiled, and that fades not away, reserved in heaven for you, who are kept by the power of God through faith to salvation ready to be revealed in the last time.
(1 Peter 1:3–5)

SEEKING/WAITING ON GOD

If from there you shall seek the LORD your God, you shall find Him, if you seek Him with all your heart and with all your soul.
(Deuteronomy 4:29)

Therefore will the LORD wait, that He may be gracious to you, and therefore will He be exalted, that He may have mercy upon you: for the LORD is a God of judgment: blessed are all they that wait for Him.
(Isaiah 30:18)

They that wait upon the LORD shall renew their strength; they shall mount up with wings as eagles; they shall run, and not be weary; and they shall walk, and not faint.
(Isaiah 40:31)

And you shall seek Me, and find Me, when you shall search for Me with all your heart. And I will be found of you, says the LORD.
(Jeremiah 29:13–14)

The LORD is good to them that wait for Him, to the soul that seeks Him. It is good that a man should both hope and quietly wait for the salvation of the LORD. (Lamentations 3:25–26)

But seek you first the kingdom of God, and His righteousness; and all these things shall be added to you.   (Matthew 6:33)

He that comes to God must believe that He is, and that He is a rewarder of them that diligently seek Him.   (Hebrews 11:6)

PEACE

The LORD will give strength to His people; the LORD will bless His people with peace.   (Psalm 29:11)

But the meek shall inherit the earth; and shall delight themselves in the abundance of peace.   (Psalm 37:11)

You will keep him in perfect peace, whose mind is stayed on You: because he trusts in You.   (Isaiah 26:3)

Peace I leave with you, My peace I give to you: not as the world gives, give I to you. Let not your heart be troubled, neither let it be afraid.   (John 14:27)

Therefore being justified by faith, we have peace with God through our Lord Jesus Christ: by whom also we have access by faith into this grace wherein we stand, and rejoice in hope of the glory of God.... Much more then, being now justified by His blood, we shall be saved from wrath through Him.
(Romans 5:1–2, 9)

For to be carnally minded is death; but to be spiritually minded is life and peace.   (Romans 8:6)

But the fruit of the Spirit is love, joy, peace, long-suffering, gentleness, goodness, faith, meekness, temperance: against such there is no law.   (Galatians 5:22–23)

Be careful [anxious] for nothing; but in every thing by prayer and supplication with thanksgiving let your requests be made known to God. And the peace of God, which passes all understanding, shall keep your hearts and minds through Christ Jesus. Finally, brethren, whatsoever things are true, whatsoever things are honest [honorable], whatsoever things are just, whatsoever things are pure, whatsoever things are lovely, whatsoever things are of good report; if there be any virtue, and if there be any praise, think on these things.

(Philippians 4:6–8)

WISDOM/GUIDANCE/REVELATION

Your word is a lamp to my feet, and a light to my path.

(Psalm 119:105)

For the LORD gives wisdom: out of His mouth comes knowledge and understanding. He lays up sound wisdom for the righteous: He is a buckler to them that walk uprightly.

(Proverbs 2:6–7)

Trust in the LORD with all your heart; and lean not to your own understanding. In all your ways acknowledge Him, and He shall direct your paths.   (Proverbs 3:5–6)

The fear of the LORD is the beginning of wisdom: and the knowledge of the holy is understanding.   (Proverbs 9:10)

Blessed be the name of God for ever and ever: for wisdom and might are His:…He gives wisdom to the wise, and knowledge to them that know understanding: He reveals the deep and secret things: He knows what is in the darkness, and the light dwells with Him.   (Daniel 2:20–22)

But of Him are you in Christ Jesus, who of God is made to us wisdom, and righteousness, and sanctification, and redemption. (1 Corinthians 1:30)

In whom [Jesus Christ] are hidden all the treasures of wisdom and knowledge. (Colossians 2:3)

If any of you lacks wisdom, he should ask God, who gives generously to all without finding fault, and it will be given to him. But when he asks, he must believe and not doubt, because he who doubts is like a wave of the sea, blown and tossed by the wind. That man should not think he will receive anything from the Lord; he is a double-minded man, unstable in all he does. (James 1:5–8 NIV)

SUFFERING/DIFFICULTIES/PERSECUTION

The LORD shall preserve you from all evil: He shall preserve your soul. (Psalm 121:7)

Blessed are they which are persecuted for righteousness' sake: for theirs is the kingdom of heaven. Blessed are you, when men shall revile you, and persecute you, and shall say all manner of evil against you falsely, for My sake. Rejoice, and be exceeding glad: for great is your reward in heaven: for so persecuted they the prophets which were before you. (Matthew 5:10–12)

We glory in tribulations [afflictions, troubles] also: knowing that tribulation works patience. (Romans 5:3)

The Spirit Himself bears witness with our spirit that we are children of God, and if children, heirs also, heirs of God and fellow heirs with Christ, if indeed we suffer with Him in order

that we may also be glorified with Him.
                              (Romans 8:16–17 NASB)

We know that all things work together for good to them that love God, to them who are the called according to His purpose.   (Romans 8:28)

For I am persuaded, that neither death, nor life, nor angels, nor principalities, nor powers, nor things present, nor things to come, nor height, nor depth, nor any other creature, shall be able to separate us from the love of God, which is in Christ Jesus our Lord.   (Romans 8:38–39)

Yea, and all that will live godly in Christ Jesus shall suffer persecution.   (2 Timothy 3:12)

Not rendering evil for evil, or railing for railing: but contrariwise blessing; knowing that you are thereunto called, that you should inherit a blessing.   (1 Peter 3:9)

TRIALS/TEMPTATIONS

There has no temptation taken you but such as is common to man: but God is faithful, who will not suffer you to be tempted above that you are able; but will with the temptation also make a way to escape, that you may be able to bear it.
                              (1 Corinthians 10:13)

For we have not a high priest which cannot be touched with the feeling of our infirmities [weaknesses]; but was in all points tempted [tested] like as we are, yet without sin. Let us therefore come boldly to the throne of grace, that we may obtain mercy, and find grace to help in time of need.
                              (Hebrews 4:15–16)

My brethren, count it all joy when you fall into divers temptations [trials, tests]; knowing this, that the trying of your faith works patience. But let patience have her perfect work, that you may be perfect and entire, wanting [lacking] nothing.

(James 1:2–4)

Blessed is the man that endures temptation [trials, tests]: for when he is tried, he shall receive the crown of life, which the Lord has promised to them that love Him.   (James 1:12)

Submit yourselves therefore to God. Resist the devil, and he will flee from you.   (James 4:7)

Wherein you greatly rejoice, though now for a season, if need be, you are in heaviness through manifold temptations [testings]: that the trial of your faith, being much more precious than of gold that perishes, though it be tried with fire, might be found to praise and honor and glory at the appearing of Jesus Christ.   (1 Peter 1:6–7)

PRAYER

If My people, which are called by My name, shall humble themselves, and pray, and seek My face, and turn from their wicked ways; then will I hear from heaven, and will forgive their sin, and will heal their land.   (2 Chronicles 7:14)

The righteous cry, and the Lord *hears, and delivers them out of all their troubles.*   (Psalm 34:17)

If I regard iniquity in my heart, the Lord will not hear me: but verily God has heard me; He has attended to the voice of my prayer.   (Psalm 66:18–19)

Again I say to you, that if two of you shall agree on earth as touching any thing that they shall ask, it shall be done for them of My Father which is in heaven. For where two or three are gathered together in My name, there am I in the midst of them. (Matthew 18:19–20)

Whatsoever you shall ask the Father in My name, He will give it you. Until now have you asked nothing in My name: ask, and you shall receive, that your joy may be full. (John 16:23–24)

Wives, in the same way be submissive to your husbands so that, if any of them do not believe the word, they may be won over without words by the behavior of their wives, when they see the purity and reverence of your lives.... Husbands, in the same way be considerate as you live with your wives, and treat them with respect as the weaker partner and as heirs with you of the gracious gift of life, so that nothing will hinder your prayers. (1 Peter 3:1, 7 NIV)

For the eyes of the Lord are over the righteous, and His ears are open to their prayers. (1 Peter 3:12)

Beloved, if our heart condemn us not, then have we confidence toward God. And whatsoever we ask, we receive of Him, because we keep His commandments, and do those things that are pleasing in His sight. (1 John 3:21–22)

This is the confidence that we have in Him, that, if we ask any thing according to His will, He hears us: and if we know that He hear us, whatsoever we ask, we know that we have the petitions that we desired of Him. (1 John 5:14–15)

MARRIAGE/CHILDREN

Then the Lord *God said, "It is not good for the man to be alone; I will make him a helper suitable for him."*
(Genesis 2:18 NASB)

But the mercy ["love" NIV] of the Lord is from everlasting to everlasting upon them that fear Him, and His righteousness to children's children; to such as keep His covenant, and to those that remember His commandments to do them.
(Psalm 103:17–18)

Blessed is the man that fears the Lord, *that delights greatly in His commandments. His seed [offspring] shall be mighty upon earth: the generation of the upright shall be blessed. Wealth and riches shall be in His house: and His righteousness endures for ever.*   (Psalm 112:1–3)

Whoso finds a wife finds a good thing, and obtains favor of the Lord.   (Proverbs 18:22)

Houses and wealth are inherited from parents, but a prudent wife is from the Lord.   (Proverbs 19:14 NIV)

Shall the prey be taken from the mighty, or the lawful captive delivered? But thus says the Lord, *Even the captives of the mighty shall be taken away, and the prey of the terrible [ruthless] shall be delivered: for I will contend with him that contends with you, and I will save your children.*
(Isaiah 49:24–25)

Thus says the Lord; *A voice was heard in Ramah, lamentation, and bitter weeping; Rachel weeping for her children refused to be comforted for her children, because they were not.*

Thus says the LORD; *Refrain your voice from weeping, and your eyes from tears: for your work shall be rewarded, says the* LORD; *and they [your children] shall come again from the land of the enemy. And there is hope in your end, says the* LORD, *that your children shall come again to their own border.* (Jeremiah 31:15–17)

Behold, I will send you Elijah the prophet before the coming of the great and dreadful day of the LORD: *and he shall turn the heart of the fathers to the children, and the heart of the children to their fathers, lest I come and smite the earth with a curse.* (Malachi 4:5–6)

Children, obey your parents in the Lord: for this is right. Honor your father and mother; (which is the first commandment with promise;) that it may be well with you, and you may live long on the earth. And, you fathers, provoke not your children to wrath: but bring them up in the nurture and admonition of the Lord. (Ephesians 6:1–4)

ABUNDANCE/FRUITFULNESS

For I will have respect to you, and make you fruitful, and multiply you, and establish My covenant with you. And you shall eat old store, and bring forth the old because of the new. (Leviticus 26:9–10)

And it shall come to pass, if you shall hearken diligently to the voice of the LORD *your God, to observe and to do all His commandments which I command you this day, that the* LORD *your God will set you on high above all nations of the earth: and all these blessings shall come on you, and overtake you, if you shall hearken to the voice of the* LORD *your God.... And the* LORD *shall make you plenteous in goods, in the fruit of your body, and in the fruit of your cattle, and in the fruit of your ground, in the land which the* LORD *swore to your fathers to give you. The* LORD *shall open to you His good treasure, the heaven to give the rain to your land in its season, and to bless all the work of your hand.*   (Deuteronomy 28:1–2, 11–12)

For the LORD *God is a sun and shield: the* LORD *will give grace and glory: no good thing will He withhold from them that walk uprightly.*   (Psalm 84:11)

I am come that they might have life, and that they might have it more abundantly.   (John 10:10)

Abide in Me, and I in you. As the branch cannot bear fruit of itself, except it abide in the vine; no more can you, except you abide in Me. I am the vine, you are the branches: he that abides in Me, and I in him, the same brings forth much fruit: for without Me you can do nothing.... If you abide in Me, and My words abide in you, you shall ask what you will, and it shall be done to you. Herein is My Father glorified, that you bear much fruit; so shall you be My disciples.
(John 15:4–5, 7–8)

He that spared not His own Son, but delivered Him up for us all, how shall He not with Him also freely give us all things?
(Romans 8:32)

PROSPERITY/SUCCESS

And the LORD *shall make you the head and not the tail; and you shall be above only, and you shall not be beneath; if that you hearken to the commandments of the* LORD *your God.*
(Deuteronomy 28:13)

Keep therefore the words of this covenant, and do them, that you may prosper in all that you do.   (Deuteronomy 29:9)

This book of the law shall not depart out of your mouth but you shall meditate therein day and night, that you may observe to do according to all that is written therein: for then you shall make your way prosperous, and then you shall have good success.   (Joshua 1:8)

Blessed is the man that walks not in the counsel of the ungodly, nor stands in the way of sinners, nor sits in the seat of the scornful. But his delight is in the law of the LORD; and in His law does he meditate day and night. And he shall be like a tree planted by the rivers of water, that brings forth his fruit in his season; his leaf also shall not wither; and whatsoever he does shall prosper.   (Psalm 1:1–3)

Delight yourself also in the LORD; and He shall give you the desires of your heart. Commit your way to the LORD; trust also in Him; and He shall bring it to pass.   (Psalm 37:4–5)

Blessed is every one that fears the LORD; that walks in His ways. For you shall eat the labor of your hands: happy shall you be, and it shall be well with you.   (Psalm 128:1–2)

HEALING/HEALTH

If you will diligently hearken to the voice of the LORD your God, and will do that which is right in His sight, and will give ear to His commandments, and keep all His statutes, I will put none of these diseases upon you, which I have brought upon the Egyptians: for I am the LORD that heals you ["I, the LORD, am your healer" NASB].   (Exodus 15:26)

*Fools because of their transgression, and because of their iniq-
uities, are afflicted. Their soul abhors all manner of meat;
and they draw near to the gates of death. Then they cry to
the* LORD *in their trouble, and He saves them out of their
distresses. He sent His word, and healed them, and delivered
them from their destructions.*   (Psalm 107:17–20)

*My son, attend to my words; incline your ear to my sayings.
Let them not depart from your eyes; keep them in the midst of
your heart. For they are life to those that find them, and health
to all their flesh.*   (Proverbs 4:20–22)

Surely He has borne our griefs, and carried our sorrows
[more literally, "our pains"]: *yet we did esteem Him stricken,
smitten of God, and afflicted. But He was wounded for our
transgressions, He was bruised for our iniquities: the chastise-
ment of our peace was upon Him; and with His stripes we
are healed. All we like sheep have gone astray; we have turned
every one to his own way; and the* LORD *has laid on Him the
iniquity of us all.*   (Isaiah 53:4–6)

*When the evening was come, they brought to Him many that
were possessed with devils* [demons]: *and He cast out the spirits with His word, and healed all that were sick: that it might
be fulfilled which was spoken by Isaiah the prophet, saying,
Himself took our infirmities, and bore our sicknesses.*
          (Matthew 8:16–17)

*And His name through faith in His name has made this man
strong, whom you see and know: yea, the faith which is by
Him has given him this perfect soundness* ["healing" NIV] *in
the presence of you all.*   (Acts 3:16)

But if the Spirit of Him that raised up Jesus from the dead dwell in you, He that raised up Christ from the dead shall also quicken ["give life to" NASB, NIV, NKJV] your mortal bodies by His Spirit that dwells in you.   (Romans 8:11)

Is any sick among you? let him call for the elders of the church; and let them pray over him, anointing him with oil in the name of the Lord: and the prayer of faith shall save [heal] the sick, and the Lord shall raise him up; and if he have committed sins, they shall be forgiven him. Confess your faults one to another, and pray one for another, that you may be healed. The effectual fervent prayer of a righteous man avails much.
(James 5:14–16)

Who His own self bore our sins in His own body on the tree, that we, being dead to sins, should live to righteousness: by whose stripes you were healed.   (1 Peter 2:24)

Beloved, I wish above all things that you may prosper and be in health, even as your soul prospers.   (3 John 2)

MATERIAL PROVISION

O fear the LORD, you His saints: for there is no want [lack] to them that fear Him. The young lions do lack, and suffer hunger: but they that seek the LORD shall not want any good thing.   (Psalm 34:9–10)

Honor the LORD with your substance [wealth], and with the first-fruits of all your increase: so shall your barns be filled with plenty, and your presses shall burst out with new wine.
(Proverbs 3:9–10)

There is that scatters ["gives freely" NIV], and yet increases; and there is that withholds more than is meet, but it tends to poverty. The liberal soul shall be made fat: and he that waters shall be watered also himself.   (Proverbs 11:24–25)

Bring you all the tithes into the storehouse, that there may be meat in My house, and prove Me now herewith, says the LORD of hosts, if I will not open you the windows of heaven, and pour you out a blessing, that there shall not be room enough to receive it. And I will rebuke the devourer for your sakes, and he shall not destroy the fruits of your ground; neither shall your vine cast her fruit before the time in the field, says the LORD of hosts. And all nations shall call you blessed: for you shall be a delightful land, says the LORD of hosts.   (Malachi 3:10–12)

But this I say, he which sows sparingly shall reap also sparingly; and he which sows bountifully shall reap also bountifully. Every man according as he purposed in his heart, so let him give; not grudgingly, or of necessity: for God loves a cheerful giver. And God is able to make all grace abound toward you; that you, always having all sufficiency in all things, may abound to every good work.   (2 Corinthians 9:6–8)

My God shall supply all your need according to His riches in glory by Christ Jesus.   (Philippians 4:19)

WORK/BUSINESS

My son, forget not my law; but let your heart keep my commandments: for length of days, and long life, and peace, shall they add to you. Let not mercy and truth forsake you: bind them about your neck; write them upon the table of your heart: so shall you find favor and good understanding ["high esteem" NKJV] in the sight of God and man.

(Proverbs 3:1–4)

Wealth gotten by vanity shall be diminished: but he that gathers by labor shall increase. (Proverbs 13:11)

The thoughts ["plans" NASB, NIV, NKJV] of the diligent tend only to plenteousness; but of every one that is hasty only to want ["poverty" NASB, NIV, NKJV]. (Proverbs 21:5)

See you a man diligent in his business? he shall stand before kings. (Proverbs 22:29)

A faithful man will abound with blessings, but he who makes haste to be rich will not go unpunished.

(Proverbs 28:20 NASB)

For the kingdom of God is not meat and drink; but righteousness, and peace, and joy in the Holy Ghost [Spirit]. For he that in these things serves Christ is acceptable to God, and approved of men. (Romans 14:17–18)

Servants, be obedient to them that are your masters according to the flesh, with fear and trembling, in singleness of your heart, as to Christ; not with eye-service, as men-pleasers; but as the servants of Christ, doing the will of God from the heart; with good will doing service, as to the Lord, and not to men: knowing that whatsoever good thing any man does, the same shall he receive of the Lord, whether he be bond or free.

(Ephesians 6:5–8)

ABOUT THE AUTHOR

Derek Prince (1915–2003) was born in India of British parents. He was educated as a scholar of Greek and Latin at Eton College and King's College, Cambridge, in England. Upon graduation, he held a fellowship (equivalent to a professorship) in Ancient and Modern Philosophy at King's College. Prince also studied Hebrew, Aramaic, and modern languages at Cambridge and the Hebrew University in Jerusalem. As a student, he was a philosopher and a self-proclaimed agnostic.

While serving in the Royal Army Medical Corps (RAMC) during World War II, Prince began to study the Bible as a philosophical work. Converted through a powerful encounter with Jesus Christ, he was baptized in the Holy Spirit a few days later. Out of this encounter, he formed two conclusions: first, that Jesus Christ is alive; second, that the Bible is a true, relevant, up-to-date book. These conclusions altered the whole course of his life, which he then devoted to studying and teaching the Bible as the Word of God.

Discharged from the army in Jerusalem in 1945, he married Lydia Christensen, founder of a children's home there. Upon their marriage, he immediately became father to Lydia's eight adopted daughters—six Jewish, one Palestinian Arab, and one English. Together, the family saw the rebirth of the state of Israel in 1948. In the late 1950s, they adopted another daughter while Prince was serving as principal of a teachers' training college in Kenya.

In 1963, the Princes immigrated to the United States and pastored a church in Seattle. In 1973, Prince became one of the founders of Intercessors for America. His book *Shaping History through Prayer and Fasting* has awakened Christians around the world to their responsibility to pray for their governments. Many consider underground translations of the book as instrumental in the fall of communist regimes in the USSR, East Germany, and Czechoslovakia.

Lydia Prince died in 1975, and Prince married Ruth Baker (a single mother to three adopted children) in 1978. He met his second wife, like his first wife, while she was serving the Lord in Jerusalem. Ruth died in December 1998 in Jerusalem, where they had lived since 1981.

Until a few years before his own death in 2003 at the age of eighty-eight, Prince persisted in the ministry God had called him to as he traveled the world, imparting God's revealed truth, praying for the sick and afflicted, and sharing his prophetic insights into world events in the light of Scripture. Internationally recognized as a Bible scholar and spiritual patriarch, Derek Prince established a teaching ministry that spanned six continents and more than sixty years. He is the author of more than eighty books, six hundred audio teachings, and one hundred video teachings, many of which have been translated and published in more than one hundred languages. He pioneered teaching on such groundbreaking themes as generational curses, the biblical significance of Israel, and demonology.

Prince's radio program, which began in 1979, has been translated into more than a dozen languages and continues to touch lives. Derek Prince's main gift of explaining the Bible and its teachings in a clear and simple way has helped build a foundation of faith in millions of lives. His nondenominational, nonsectarian approach has made his teaching equally relevant and helpful to people from all racial and religious backgrounds, and his messages are estimated to have reached more than half the globe.

In 2002, he said, "It is my desire—and I believe the Lord's desire—that this ministry continue the work, which God began through me over sixty years ago, until Jesus returns."

Derek Prince Ministries continues to reach out to believers in over 140 countries with Derek's teaching, fulfilling the mandate to keep on "until Jesus returns." This is accomplished through the outreaches of more than forty-five Derek Prince offices around the world, including primary work in Australia, Canada, China, France, Germany, the Netherlands, New Zealand, Norway, Russia, South Africa, Switzerland, the United Kingdom, and the United States. For current information about these and other worldwide locations, visit www.derekprince.org.